- Zoological and Acclimatisation Society of Victoria

Proceedings of the Zoological and Acclimatisation Society of Victoria, and report of the annual meeting of the Society

Zoological and Acclimatisation Society of Victoria

Proceedings of the Zoological and Acclimatisation Society of Victoria, and report of the annual meeting of the Society

ISBN/EAN: 9783743355033

Manufactured in Europe, USA, Canada, Australia, Japa

Cover: Foto ©ninafisch / pixelio.de

Manufactured and distributed by brebook publishing software (www.brebook.com)

Zoological and Acclimatisation Society of Victoria

Proceedings of the Zoological and Acclimatisation Society of Victoria, and report of the annual meeting of the Society

PROCEEDINGS

OF THE

ZOOLOGICAL & ACCLIMATISATION SOCIETY OF VICTORIA.

PROCEEDINGS

OF THE

Zoological and Acclimatisation Society

OF VICTORIA,

AND

REPORT OF THE ANNUAL MEETING OF THE SOCIETY,

HELD 23RD FEBRUARY, 1874.

"*Omnis feret omnia tellus.*"

VOLUME III.

MELBOURNE:
STILLWELL AND KNIGHT, PRINTERS, COLLINS STREET EAST.
1874.

LIST OF THE OFFICERS
OF THE
Zoological & Acclimatisation Society
OF VICTORIA.

Patron:
His Excellency Sir G. F. Bowen, G.C.M.G.

President:
ALBERT PURCHAS, Esq.

Vice-Presidents:
F. R. GODFREY, Esq. | PROFESSOR STRONG.

Hon. Treasurer:
DR. JOSEPH BLACK.

Members of the Council:

CURZON ALLPORT, Esq.	CHARLES RYAN, Esq.
DR. THOMAS BLACK.	WM. ROBERTSON, Esq.
HON. J. J. CASEY.	GEORGE SPRIGG, Esq.
ROBERT HAMMOND, Esq.	H. P. VENABLES, Esq., B.A.
FREDERICK G. MOULE, Esq.	J. B. WERE, Esq.

SAMUEL WILSON, Esq.

Hon. Secretary:
ALBERT A. C. LE SOUEF, Esq.

Collector:
MR. A. O. SEGERBERG.

Hon. Veterinary Surgeon:
MR. GRAHAM MITCHELL.

Bailiff:
FRANCIS MEAKER.

OFFICE OF THE SOCIETY—60 TEMPLE COURT.

CONTENTS.

List of Officers	5
Report of the Council	9
Rules and Objects	24
List of Animals and Birds in the Zoological Gardens, Royal Park	29
List of Donors to the Zoological and Acclimatisation Society, 1873-4	30
Stock acquired during the year 1873-4, by purchase or exchange	31
Stock sold, presented, or exchanged by the Society during the year 1873-4	31
Animals liberated previous to 1870	32
Animals sent away	34
Report on the Fish Breeding Ponds	37
Additions to the Lists of Principal Timber Trees, &c., readily eligible for Victorian Culture. By Baron Ferd. von Mueller	47
Ostrich Farming. By Dr. Atherstone	96

REPORT OF THE COUNCIL.

It is with considerable satisfaction that the Council of the Zoological and Acclimatisation Society submits its Tenth Annual Report to the subscribers. The Council is glad to find the effort to establish a Zoological Garden at the Royal Park in connection with acclimatisation has met with the decided approval of the public, as evidenced by the largely increased list of members and number of visitors during the past year. The zoological collection is steadily increasing, several additions having been made since the last annual meeting. His Excellency Sir Henry Barkly has kindly undertaken to procure a pair of elands, and Mr. James McLachlan has promised to obtain some tigers from Java, for the Society. The Council is determined to lose no opportunity to extend its collection, and only requires to receive a larger subsidy or increased subscriptions to provide more suitable accommodation for the larger animals, as well as to construct a reptile house, which was contemplated last year, but which, from the necessity for artificial heat and the consequent expense, could not be carried out. The garden has also been very much improved and beautified, new walks have been opened up, and considerable additions made to the flower-beds.

The most notable work of the past year has been the construction of the trout ponds for breeding purposes at Wooling, Mount Macedon, somewhat

similar to the ponds at New Norfolk, in Tasmania.
The cost of construction was £357 11s. 11d., £300
of which amount was voted to the Society during the
last session of Parliament as a special grant for the
work. There are two ponds; one for salmon trout and
the other for brown trout. They are supplied from the
waters of Riddell's Creek, and are finished in a complete and substantial manner. The thanks of the
Council are due to Mr. Curzon Allport, one of their
body, for furnishing plans, and for the practical
interest he has taken throughout; also to Mr. Gerard
Blackburn, engineer of Gisborne, who superintended
their construction, and to Mr. William Robertson, of
Wooling, on whose property the ponds are situated,
and who has from the first taken a deep interest in
the work. The ponds are now stocked with young
fish (salmon trout and brown trout), and as soon as
these become productive it will be a comparatively
easy matter to stock all suitable streams in the
colony. The Council hears, from time to time,
of the capture of large trout in the different creeks
stocked some years since by the Society; one a
short while ago was killed, which weighed upwards
of 9 lbs.

Another work of equal importance has also been
carried to a successful issue since the last general
meeting, namely, the formation of a pheasant breeding
establishment in connection with the Society. It is
situated in the ranges, about forty miles to the south-
east of Melbourne, and so far the experiment
has succeeded admirably, the birds thriving there
remarkably well. The Council trusts that, through
its instrumentality, pheasants will before long become

abundant in the portions of the colony suited to their habits. A large number of pheasants' eggs have likewise been distributed to subscribers during the past year. The Council would here desire to record its warm thanks to its first President, Mr. Edward Wilson, who has from the first taken an interest in the game breeding farm, and contributed largely towards its expenses. Mr. Wilson has for years past been anxious to see our forests stocked with game, and it is hoped that his wish will now be realised. Mr. Wilson's munificent donation does not appear in the Society's books, as the money was given privately to the Hon. Secretary to expend.

The Society's ostriches have lately been removed to Mr. Officer's station, Murray Downs, Swan Hill, where it is thought they will thrive better than on the Wimmera, it being Mr. Officer's intention to hatch the eggs in an incubator, which he is procuring from the Cape of Good Hope, similar to that used on the ostrich farms there. The Angora goats still continue in Mr. Samuel Wilson's charge; that gentleman has lately removed them from the Wimmera to his estate of Ercildoun, near Ballarat. The flock has increased since the last annual meeting, from 108 to 173 head. Several male goats were sold during last year, and the Society has now 50 pure males for sale. The stock liberated in 1873 consists of deer; hares sent to different parts of Victoria and other colonies; pheasants, Californian quail, French partridges, and 100 English skylarks obtained from Nelson, N.Z., &c. A large number of carp and some perch and trout have also been distributed.

The Society's silver medal has been awarded to

Charles Lyall Grant, Esq., of Shanghae, and James McLachlan, Esq., late of Java, but now of Cheltenham, England; and the bronze medal to Captain Jones, of the ship *Superb*, and Mr. Millett, second officer of the P. and O. Company's steamer *Bangalore*, for services rendered to the Society. The Council is likewise much indebted to Mr. Robert Scott of the Murrumbidgee, and Mr. George E. Jemmett, second officer of the ship *Shannon*, who during the past year have brought out valuable birds from England, at considerable trouble and expense to themselves, and presented them to the Society.

The balance-sheets for the past year are laid before the meeting, showing an expenditure of £2136 18s. 11d. inclusive of the sum expended on the construction of the fish ponds. The Council feels that the success of the Society, and the satisfactory improvement in the gardens and stock, is mainly due to the Hon. Secretary, Mr. Le Souef, whose active interest and careful supervision has raised the Society to its present position in public estimation.

Before concluding this report, the Council desires to return its best thanks to Mr. Frederic R. Godfrey, for the able manner in which he has discharged the duties of President of the Society during his year of office. In conformity with rule 4, the following Members retire from the Council, being the three who have attended the fewest meetings. Messrs. J. B. Were, Robert Hammond, and Dr. Joseph Black, these gentlemen are eligible for re-election. The meeting has also to elect, by ballot, a President and two Vice-Presidents for the ensuing year.

The Chairman, in moving the adoption of the report, said that he had much pleasure in stating that since the last Annual Meeting His Excellency Sir George Bowen had consented to accept the office of Patron of the Society; and in suggesting that an addition be made to that effect, he was glad to find that the position of the Society had materially improved since the change in its constitution, made nearly two years ago (which, it was anticipated by some of the members, would prove disastrous to its prosperity and success), came into operation; and that from the improvement in the subscription list and the increased number of visitors to the gardens, it was plain that the Society stood high in the estimation of the public. This was no doubt due to the admirable manner in which the gardens had been improved and managed by the curator, and to the interesting additions made to the zoological collection. He considered that Melbourne had now reached a position of importance sufficient to render a zoological collection not only necessary but self-supporting; but at present the Society was placed in an uncertain position with respect to the Government grant, for which it depended entirely on the good will of the Members of Parliament. Though it was no doubt true that the subscription list was increasing, and the Society improving in public estimation, yet he believed it was impossible that it could maintain its present zoological collection—or indeed keep up an existence—from that source alone, without a grant from the Government; and he would like the members of the Society and those who were interested in its welfare to consider this matter, in order that steps might be taken to place the Society in a more independent position, and to make its attractions so great as to ensure its becoming at some future day self-supporting and popular, like the zoological societies of Europe.

Mr. J. B. Were seconded the motion for the adoption of the report, with the addition suggested by the Chairman, which was carried.

The Balance-sheet showed that the receipts for the past year amounted to £2,090 0s. 1d., while the expenditure, including £300 for the fish-ponds at Mount Macedon, amounted to £2,136 18s. 11d.

A ballot was then taken for the election of Office-Bearers, with the following result :—

President.
ALBERT PURCHAS, Esq.

Vice-Presidents.
F. R. GODFREY, Esq.   Professor STRONG.

Messrs. J. B. WERE, R. HAMMOND, and Dr. JOSEPH BLACK, were re-elected Members of the Council.

A cordial vote of thanks was passed to the President, Hon. Treasurer, Hon. Secretary, and other Office-Bearers, for their exertions on behalf of the Society during the past year, and the proceedings terminated.

BALANCE SHEET.

Account of Monies received and paid by the Zoological & Acclimatisation Society of Victoria.
During the period 1st January to 30th June, 1873.

RECEIPTS.	£	s.	d.	PAYMENTS.		£	s.	d.
Government Grant	500	0	0	Premises		108	19	5
Subscriptions and Donations	188	7	6	Food and Forage		177	19	6
Sale of Stock and Wool	38	17	0	Purchase and Transport of Stock		70	14	4
Cash in Hon. Secretary's hands, 1st January	5	14	10	Farming Implements, Carts, Tools, &c.		18	18	0
Balance at Bank of Victoria, 1st January	22	1	11	Wages		210	18	0
				Office Expenses		74	4	9
				Incidental Expenses		46	10	7
				Interest		0	13	11
				Cash in Hon. Secretary's hands, 30th June	£1 18 7			
				Balance at the Bank, 30th June	44 4 2	46	2	9
	£755	1	3			£755	1	3

J. BLACK, M.D., *Hon. Treasurer.*

Audited and found correct,
W. F. A. RUCKER.

Melbourne, 10th *July,* 1874.

ALBERT A. C. LE SOUEF, *Hon. Secretary.*

BALANCE SHEET.

Account of Monies received and paid by the Zoological & Acclimatisation Society of Victoria.

During the period 1st July to 31st December, 1873.

RECEIPTS.	£	s.	d.
Government Grant	1000	0	0
Subscriptions and Donations	312	1	0
Sale of Stock and Wool	49	6	6
Refund from Railway Department	1	8	1
Cash in Hon. Secretary's hands, 1st July	1	18	7
Balance at Bank of Victoria, 1st July	44	4	2
Overdraft 31st December	25	1	8
	£1,434	0	0

PAYMENTS.	£	s.	d.
Printing	226	3	8
Premises	213	15	10
Food and Forage	144	6	7
Purchase and Transport of Stock	115	0	3
Farming Implements, Carts, Tools, &c.	12	5	0
Wages	189	2	6
Office Expenses	112	13	11
Incidental Expenses	56	14	9
Trout Ponds	357	11	11
Cash in Hon. Secretary's hands, 31st December	5	19	7
	£1,434	0	0

J. BLACK, M.D., *Hon. Treasurer.*

Melbourne, 19th January, 1874.

Audited and found correct,

W. F. A. RUCKER.

ALBERT A. C. LE SOUEF, *Hon. Secretary.*

17

LIFE MEMBERS.

Aldworth and Co., Sandhurst	£10	10 0
Armitage, George, Ballarat	.. 10	10 0
Armstrong, W., Hexham..	.. 10	10 0
Alfrey, Ernest H., Fernihurst	.. 10	10 0
Ayrey, Charles, Warrauuke	.. 10	10 0
Barkly, His Excellency Sir Henry	42	0 0
Bear, Hon. J. P., M.L.C.	.. 21	0 0
Bear, Thomas H., Heidelberg	.. 10	10 0
Black, Dr. Thomas, Melbourne Club	.. 10	10 0
Black, W., Belfast ..	.. 10	10 0
Borough Council of Sandhurst	.. 10	10 0
Box, H., Little Collins-street West	.. 10	10 0
Boyd and Currie, Collins-street West	.. 10	10 0
Bright Brothers, & Co., Flinders-lane	.. 10	10 0
Brown, Lindsay, Garramadda, Wahgunyah	.. 10	10 0
Canterbury, His Excellency Viscount	.. 10	10 0
Campbell, Finlay, Raywood	.. 10	10 0
Catto, John, Newbridge, Loddon	10	10 0
Chambers, H. J., St. Kilda	..	Services
Cooper, Sir Daniel, London	.. 37	2 0
Coppin, G. S., Richmond..	.. 10	10 0
Creswick, Borough Council of	.. 10	10 0
Cumming, G., Mount Fyans	.. 10	10 0
Cumming, W., Toorak ..	.. 10	10 0
Curr, E. M., Queen-street	.. 10	10 0
Dalgety and Co, Little Collins-street	.. 10	10 0
Docker, F. G., Wangaratta	.. 10	10 0
Edols, John, Ingleston ..	.. 10	10 0
Falconer., J. J., Bank of Australasia	.. 20	0 0
Fellows, The Hon. T. H. ..	.. 10	10 0
Firebrace, R. T. ..	.. 10	10 0
Fraser, Simon, Cornelian Creek	.. 10	10 0
Fussell, R. S. R., Fou Chou dols. 50 ..	.. 11	0 10
Glass, R. J., Waiparella ..	.. 10	10 0
Hervey, The Hon. M.	.. 10	10 0
Hoffmann, W., Bush Back, Essendon	.. 25	0 0
Highett, Miss	.. 10	10 0
Jamieson, Hugh	.. 10	10 0
Jenner, Hon. C. J., M.L.C.	£10	10 0
Jones, Lloyd, Avenel	.. 10	10 0
Joshua Bros., William-street	.. 10	10 0
Lyster, W. S., Melbourne	.. 10	10 0
Landells, G. J., Lahore, India	..	Services
Layard, C. P., Colombo ..	.	Services
Layard, E. L., Cape Town	..	Services
Learmonth, Thomas, Ercibdanriley, Portland..	.. 10	10 0
Londesborough, The Right Honorable Lord, Carlton Gardens, London..	.. 37	10 0
Lyall, W.	.. 10	10 0
McEachern, D., Kangaroo	.. 10	10 0
Mein, G. A., Moolpa, N.S.W.	.. 10	10 0
Mackinnon, L., "Argus" Office		Services
Mackenzie, John ..	.. 10	10 0
Macintosh, Alexander ..	.. 10	10 0
Marshall, Captain D. S. ..	..	Services
Martin, Dr., Heidelberg ..	.. 10	10 0
Matheson, J., Bank of Victoria	.. 21	0 0
McGill, A.	.. 10	10 0
McGregor, Samuel, Belfast	.. 10	10 0
McHaffie, John, Phillip Island	.. 10	10 0
McMullen, J., Union Bank	.. 21	0 0
McKellar, Hon. T., M.L.C.	.. 10	10 0
Molloy, W. T., Hawthorn	.. 10	10 0
Mueller, Baron Von, Botanic Gardens	.. 10	10 0
Municipal Council of Ballarat W.	20	0 0
Murray, S., Dunrobin ..	.. 10	10 0
Nicholson, Germain, Collins-street East	.. 10	10 0
Officer, C. M., Brighton ..	.. 10	10 0
Officer, S. H., Murray Downs, N.S.W. ..	.. 10	10 0
Officer, W., Zara, N.S.W...	.. 10	10 0
Purchas, Albert, Kew ..	..	Services
Ritchie, J., Streatham ..	.. 10	10 0
Rostron, John R., Navarre	.. 10	10 0
Rusden, G. W., Brighton..	.. 10	10 0
Russell, A., Matuwalloch..	.. 10	10 0
Rutledge, William, Belfast	.. 10	10 0
Salmon, J., E. S. and A. C. Bank	£1	0 0
Sargood, King and Sargood, Flinders-street	.. 10	10 0
Shoobridge, E., Valleyfield, Tasmania	.. 10	10 0

C

ANNUAL MEMBERS.

	£ s d		£ s d
Simpson, Hon. Robert, Toorak	10 10 0	Youl, James, A., Clapham Park, London	Services
Sladen, Hon. C., Birregurra	10 10 0		
Sloan, W. S., Fou Chou, dols. 50	11 0 10	**LIFE MEMBERS, 1873.**	
Spowers, Allan, "Argus" Office	10 10 0		
Stanbridge, W. E., Daylesford	10 10 0	Amess, Samuel, William-street	10 10 0
Staughton, S. T., Little Collins-street West	10 10 0	Bushell, C., Chiltern	10 10 0
		Bowen, His Excellency Sir George	10 10 0
Strachan, J., London Chartered Bank	21 0 0	Calvert, John, Colac	10 10 0
		Currie, J. L., Lara..	10 10 0
Stewart, J., Emerdale, Streatham	21 0 0	Chirnside, A., Werribee Park	10 10 0
Sumner, T. J., 24 Flinders-lane West	10 10 0	Fleming, J. W., Brunswick	10 10 0
		Fisher, C. B., St. Kilda	10 10 0
Taylor, W., Overnewton, Keilor	10 10 0	Henty, Edward, St. Kilda road	10 10 0
Templeton, Hugh, Fitzroy	Services	Latham, E., Carlton Brewery	10 10 0
Ware, Joseph, Caramut	10 10 0	Murphy, J. R., St. Kilda road	1 1 10 0
Wilson and Mackinnon, Collins-street East	42 0 0	North Eastern Agricultural and Horticultural Society	10 10 0
Wilson, Edward, "Argus" Office	21 0 0	Shaw, Thos., jun., Camperdown	10 10 0
Wilson, Samuel, Wimmera	10 10 0	Ware, J., Yalla-y-Poora	10 10 0
Winter, James, Toolamba, Murchison	10 10 0	Winter, W., Stanhope	10 10 0
		Wilson, John, Woodlands	10 10 0
Winter, Thomas, Winchelsea	10 10 0	Wilson, John, Gala, Lismore	10 10 0
Winter, S. P.	10 10 0	Watson, J. B., Sandhurst..	10 10 0

ANNUAL MEMBERS.

	£ s d		£ s d
Anderson and Wright, Flinders-lane	1 1 0	Black, Dr. J., Bourke-street	2 2 0
Aitkins, Thos.	1 1 0	Bright Bros., Flinders-lane	1 1 0
Anderson, A., Wallaloo	1 1 0	Blair, Jas., Toorak	1 1 0
Adam, J. (of Lawrence and Adam) William-street	1 1 0	Bury, Leech and Co., Queen-street	2 2 0
		Barry, D. M., Brunswick	1 1 0
Alcock and Co., Russell-street	1 1 0	Benn, J., Flinders-lane	1 1 0
Atkin, C. A., Hotham	1 1 0	Bindon, Judge, St. Kilda	1 1 0
Alexander, T. B., Frankfurt House, Abbotsford	1 1 0	Buckley and Nunn, Bourke-street	2 2 0
		Barwise, John, Elizabeth-street	1 1 0
Allport, C., Chancery-lane	1 1 0	Bowyer, E., Cheaveley	1 1 0
Adams, J. and W., St. Enochs	2 2 0	Buckley, E., Newbridge	1 1 0
Allen, J., Crusoe	1 1 0	Beaney, Dr. J. G., Collins-street	1 1 0
Aspinall, G. Sandhurst	1 1 0	Breese, J. C., Brunswick	1 1 0
Australian Mortgage Land and Finance Company	2 2 0	Booth, S. B., Kyneton	2 0 0
		Blair, W. G., Kyneton	1 1 0
Borough Council Kilmore	2 2 0	Bell, J., Garden Gully, Sandhurst	1 1 0
Banks, Bros., Bell & Co., Flinders-lane	2 2 0	Buckley, J., Sandhurst	1 1 0
Briscoe and Co., Collins-street	2 2 0	Buncle, J., Hotham	1 1 0
Blair, Dr., President of the Medical Society, Collins-street	1 1 0	Bligh and Harbottle, Flinders-lane	2 2 0
		Crosby, W., and Co., Queen-street	1 1 0
Bates, Hon. W., M.L.A.	1 1 0	Clarke, W., and Co., Elizabeth-st.	1 1 0
Baines, E., Little Collins-street	2 2 0	Carter, E., Collins-street	1 1 0

ANNUAL MEMBERS.

Name	£	s	d	Name	£	s	d
Cornwell, A., Brunswick	£1	1	0	Gurner, H. F., Crown Solicitor	£1	1	0
Cumming, Hon. J., M.L.C., Toorak	2	2	0	Godfrey, F. R., M.L.A., Mt. Riddley	1	1	0
Clarke, J. L., Elizabeth-street	1	1	0	Green, J. R. & Co., Gertrude-street	2	2	0
Chenery, Alfred, Delatite	2	2	0	Graham, Hon. James, M.L.C.,			
Chenery, Mrs., Delatite	2	2	0	Little Collins-street	1	1	0
Chomley, A. W., Temple-court	1	1	0	Gordon and Gotch, Collins-street	1	1	0
Cleeland, J., Bourke-street	1	1	0	Godfrey, W., Collins-street	1	1	0
Carson, John, Collins-street	1	1	0	Gordon, G., C.E., Collins-street	1	1	0
Cuthbert, Henry, Ballarat	1	1	0	Gunn, William, Kangaroo Flat	1	1	0
Clendinning, Dr., Ballarat	1	1	0	Grice, R., Flinders-lane	1	1	0
Christie, L. S., Ballarat	1	1	0	Hickling, F. J., Warrnambool	1	1	0
Campbell, Jas., Ballarat	1	1	0	Howitt, Dr. Godfrey, Caulfield	1	1	0
Catto, J., Collins-street	1	1	0	Haddon, F. W., "Argus" Office	2	2	0
Clarke, W. J., Collins-street	2	2	0	Hunt, Thos., Kilmore	1	1	0
Croaker, Scott, & Co., Collins-street	1	1	0	Highett, Hon. W., M.L.C.,			
Craine, Thos., Princes Bridge	1	1	0	Richmond	2	2	0
Campbell, Allan, Brighton	2	2	0	Haige, H., Elizabeth-street	1	1	0
Cock, Robert, Kyneton	1	1	0	Henderson, T., Royal Park	1	1	0
Clothier, S., Eaglehawk	1	1	0	Harper, R., Flinders-street	1	1	0
Caldwell, J. T., Eaglehawk	1	1	0	Heath, R. M , Kilmore	1	1	0
Currie, George, Kaarimba	1	1	0	Hughes, J., Lonsdale-street	1	1	0
Canterbury, His Excellency Viscount	10	0	0	House, Samuel, and Co., Queen-st.	2	2	0
				Hunt, Dr. Brunswick-street	1	1	0
Daley, John, Spring-street	1	1	0	Hyne, J. F., Royal Park	1	1	0
Danks, John, Bourke-street	1	1	0	Halstead and Kerr, Elizabeth-st.	1	1	0
De Beer, S., Queen-street	1	1	0	Ham, C. J. and T., Swanston-st.	1	1	0
De Pass Brothers, Collins-street	1	1	0	Hudson, Dr., Ballarat	1	1	0
Dight, W. S., Albury	1	1	0	Hepburne, B., Ballarat	1	1	0
Edwards, H., Bourke-street	1	1	0	Hurry, H., Kyneton	1	1	0
Evans, G., "Argus" Office	2	2	0	Hardy, Alex., Kyneton	1	1	0
Ellis, Joseph, Royal Park	1	1	0	Hinsby, T. G., Kyneton	1	1	0
Elliott, G., Kangaroo Flat	1	1	0	Holdsworth, J., Sandhurst	1	1	0
Fynn, J., Kilmore	1	1	0	Helm, J. A. C., Sandhurst	1	1	0
Fleetwood, T. P., Chancery-lane	1	1	0	Horwood, Jool, Sandhurst	1	1	0
Fanning, Nankivell and Co., Flinders-street	2	2	0	Hoffmeyer, C. H., Sandhurst	1	1	0
Foy, Mark, Smith-street	1	1	0	Hay, A. and J. H., Eaglehawk	1	1	0
Fitch and French, Flinders-lane	1	1	0	Hadley, J. C., Sandhurst	1	1	0
Findlay, J., Towong	2	2	0	Hall, Sam., Strathulloch	1	1	0
Foxcroft, John, Elizabeth-street	1	1	0	Hart, H. J., Queen-street	1	1	0
Fiskin, A., Queen-street	1	1	0	Inglis, Daniel, Flinders-street	1	1	0
Fairchild, J. R., William-street	1	1	0	Ingamells, J., Royal Park	1	1	0
Fraser, Hon. Alex., M.L.C., Collins-street	1	1	0	Irving, J. L. and Co., Elizabeth-street	1	1	0
Fletcher, G. A., Sandhurst	1	1	0	Jacobs, F., and Co., Queen-street	1	1	0
Frow, George, Royal Park	1	1	0	Johnston, E., Elizabeth-street	1	1	0
Froggatt, G. W., Sandhurst	1	1	0	James, Dr., Collins-street	1	1	0
Goldsborough, R., and Co., Bourke-street West	2	2	0	Joshua Bros., William-street	2	2	0
				Jones, H., Gold Broker, Sandhurst	1	1	0
Grimwood, Thos. S., Elizabeth-street	1	1	0	Jackson, Henry, Sandhurst	1	1	0
				Jackson, George H., Sandhurst	1	1	0
Gray, C., Nareeb Nareeb	2	2	0	King, S. G., Hotham	2	2	0
Gunst, Dr., Collins-street	1	1	0	Kinnear, R. H., Lower Moira	1	1	0
Grant, John, Collins-street	1	1	0	Keep, E., Elizabeth-street	1	1	0
				Kronheimer C. E., Queen-street	1	1	0

C 2

Name	£	s	d
Knochenhauer, C. E., Swanston-street	£1	1	0
King, A. H., Ballarat East		1	1	0
Kelly, M. F., Bridgewater		1	1	0
Knight, A. H., Korougah		1	1	0
Kininmonth, Jas., Barunah Plains	1	1	0
Koighley, E., Golden-square, Sandhurst		1	1	0
Kirkwood, H., Eaglehawk		1	1	0
Larnach, J. M., Kilmore		1	1	0
Long, D. R., Bourke-street		1	1	0
Lee, B., Bourke-street		2	2	0
Lindley, A. B., Royal Park		1	1	0
Lambert, T. Lonsdale-street		1	1	0
Lawrence, J. B. (of Lawrence and Adam), William-street		1	1	0
Lang, T., and Co., Elizabeth-street	1	1	0
Learmonth, W., Ballarat		1	1	0
Lister, Charles, Bourke-street		1	1	0
Lewis, W., Beaufort		1	1	0
Longford, Dr., Kyneton		1	1	0
Lansell, George, Sandhurst		1	1	0
Laing and Webster, Flinders-lane	1	1	0
Le Poor Trench, Ballarat		1	1	0
Lewis and Tait, Sandhurst		1	1	0
M'Ilwraith, John, Little Collins-st.	1	1	0
M'Naughton, Love and Co., Flinders-lane		1	1	0
McDougall, C., Brunswick		1	1	0
McCoy, Professor, University		1	1	0
McCulloch, Sellar and Co., Queen-st.	2	2	0
McLean, N. and Son., Swanston-st.	1	1	0
McEwan, Jas., and Co., Elizabeth-street		1	1	0
McFarland, R., Bourke-street		1	1	0
McDougall, Jas., Carlton		1	1	0
McVean, John, Poliah		1	1	0
McKellar, Hon. Thos., M.L.C., St. Kilda-road		5	0	0
McPherson and Co., Sandhurst		1	1	0
McIntyre, J., Sandhurst		1	1	0
Mackay and Co., Sandhurst		1	1	0
Malleson and England, Queen-st.	1	1	0
Murphy, E. J., William-street		1	1	0
Martin, G., and Co., Market-street	2	2	0
Martin, P. J., Flinders-lane		1	1	0
Matheson, J., Collins-street		1	1	0
Moule, F. G., Market-street		1	1	0
Martin, T., Brunswick		1	1	0
Mannallack, T., Brunswick		1	1	0
Maplestone, H., Royal Park		2	2	0
Muir, W. P., Collins-street		1	1	0
Michaelis, M., Lonsdale-street		1	1	0
Myers, J., and Son, Cairnbank		1	1	0
Munckton, J. R., Coliban Estate	£1	1	0
Maguirie and Cohen, Conally, N.S.W.		2	2	0
Murphy, J. R., St. Kilda-road		2	2	0
Moloney, Dr., Lonsdale-street		1	1	0
Moorhead, Captain, Sandhurst		1	1	0
Macgillivray, Dr., Sandhurst		1	1	0
Mann, J. R., and Son, Eaglehawk	1	1	0
Matheison, J., Eaglehawk		1	1	0
Moore Bros., Sandhurst		1	1	0
Nelson, Jones J., Sandhurst		1	1	0
Newell and Co., Collins-street		1	1	0
Nicholson, Germain, Collins-street	1	1	0
O'Connor, J. D., Kilmore		1	1	0
Overend, Best, Royal Park		1	1	0
Oldfield, L., Royal Park		1	1	0
Oddie, Jas., Ballarat		1	1	0
Oliver, John, Reedy Lake		2	2	0
Oliver, R., Coliban Park		1	1	0
Perry, John, Lonsdale-street		1	1	0
Paterson, W., and Co., Queen-st.	1	1	0
Power, T. H., Collins-street		1	1	0
Paterson, Ray, Palmer and Co., Flinders-lane		2	2	0
Pearson, A. O., Flinders-street		1	1	0
Paterson, W., Collins-street		1	1	0
Plummer, Dr., Sandridge		1	1	0
Piers, R. K., Kyneton		1	1	0
Ploos Van Amstel, J. W., Collins-st.	1	1	0
Ryan and Hammond, Bourke-street	2	2	0
Rocke, W. H., Collins-street		1	1	0
Rosser, Charles, Brunswick		2	2	0
Robertson, George, Little Collins-st.	1	1	0
Rudall, J. T., F.R.C.S., Collins-st.	1	1	0
Rucker, W. F. A., Collins-street		1	1	0
Rudd, A. P., Flemington		2	2	0
Rosier, J. W., Elizabeth-street		1	1	0
Rosser, E., Brunswick		1	1	0
Robertson, W., M.L.A.		2	2	0
Robertson, W., Wooling		1	1	0
Roberts, J. S., Sandhurst		1	1	0
Reade, George, Eaglehawk		1	1	0
Rowe, Dr. J. P., Mount Battery	2	2	0
Ross, Henderson and Fick, Sandhurst		1	1	0
Skene, Hon. W., M.L.C., Toorak	2	2	0
Scott, J. R., Sandhurst		1	1	0
Sprigg, W. G., Market-street		1	1	0
Spurling, W., Kilmore		1	1	0
Stevenson and Elliott, Lonsdale-st.	1	1	0
Sloane, W. and Co., Collins street	1	1	0
Sargood and Son, Flinders-street	2	2	0
Sands and M'Dougall, Collins-st.	2	2	0
Sanderson, J., and Co., William-st.	1	1	0

HONORARY MEMBERS.

	£	s	d
Stanford and Co., Bourke-street	£1	1	0
Smith, C. and J., Albert-street		1	1	0
Sprigg, George, St. Kilda		1	1	0
Steavenson, J., Railway Department	2	2	0
Smale, A. W., Queen-street	2	2	0
Simson, Hon. R., M.L.C., Toorak	2	2	0
Straw, T., Brunswick		1	1	0
Swallow and Ariell, Sandridge		1	1	0
Strong, Professor, University		1	1	0
Somner, W., Swanston-street		1	1	0
Staughton, H., Exford		1	1	0
Smith, George, Ballarat		1	1	0
Sharp, John, Collins-street		1	1	0
Shuter, Charles, P.M., Greendale		1	1	0
Stillwell and Knight, 78 Collins-street east		1	1	0
Salmon, J., Collins-street		1	1	0
Sanders, J. T., Sandhurst		1	1	0
Sayer, Charles, Sandhurst		1	1	0
Smith and Robertson, Sandhurst	1	1	0
Steward, J., Eaglehawk		1	1	0
Thomas, J., Kilmore		1	1	0
Taylor, T. H., Chancery-lane		1	1	0
Twentyman, R., Flinders-street		1	1	0
Twentyman, T., Emerald Hill		1	1	0
Terry, A., Royal Park		1	1	0
Thomson, C. J., P.M., Kyneton		1	1	0
Taylor, J., Stone Granite Works, Sandhurst		1	1	0
Thunder, A., Sandhurst	£1	1	0
Trumble, H., Eaglehawk		1	1	0
Tipper, W., Sandhurst		1	1	0
Tipper, J. R., Sandhurst		1	1	0
Taylor, Jas., California gully		1	1	0
Vahland and Getzschman, Sandhurst		1	1	0
Venables, H. P., Education Office	1	1	0
Wilson, H., Kilmore		1	1	0
Woods, John, Smith-street		1	1	0
Watson, George, Burnett-street, St. Kilda		1	1	0
Wilson, Edward, "Argus" Office	2	2	0
Welch, Henry P., Queen-street		1	1	0
Wilshin and Leighton, William-st.		1	1	0
Watkins, W., M.L.A., Gertrude-st.	1	1	0
Wood, J., and Son, Wellington-st.	1	1	0
Whitney, Chambers & Co., Swanston street		1	1	0
White, J. H., Collins-street		1	1	0
Wilson, Dr. J. P., Cragieburn		1	1	0
Watson, Thomas, Swanston-street	1	1	0
Watson, Thomas, Garden Gully, Sandhurst		1	1	0
Watson, John, Garden Gully, Sandhurst		1	1	0
Wells, G. E., Sandhurst		1	1	0
Weddell, J. G., Sandhurst		1	1	0
Wakley, R. S., Sandhurst		1	1	0

HONORARY MEMBERS.

Allport, Morton, Hobart Town.
Blanchard, W., Collins Street West.
Bouton, A., Yahoue, New Caledonia.
Buckland, Dr. F., London.
Chalmers, Dr., New Zealand.
Cleeland, J., Albion Hotel, Bourke-street.
Coste, Professor, Huningue.
Drouyn, de Lhuys, Paris.
Francis, Francis, London.
Gillanders & Arbuthnot, Calcutta.
Godfrey, Captain J. B.
Grote, Arthur, Calcutta.
Howitt, Ed.
Johnston, Clement, Crown Lands Office.
Jones, Captain, "Superb."
Madden, Walter, Office of Mines.
Mathieu, A., Yahoue, New Caledonia.
Merryman, Captain, "Essex."

Michaelis, Moritz, Elizabeth Street.
Michael, Major, Madras.
McQueen, Captain, "Martha Birnie."
Mullick, Rajendro, Calcutta.
Officer, Sir Robert, Hobart Town.
Ramel, Monsieur, Paris.
Ridgers, Captain, "Sussex."
Robinson, J., Calcutta.
Salt, Sir Titus, Saltaire, England.
Scholstein, Adolp., Flinders Lane West.
Sclater, Dr. P. L., London.
Shinner, Captain, "Northumberland."
Smith, Captain, "Dover Castle."
Squire, Surgeon John, Dinapore.
St. Hilaire, G., Bois de Boulogne, Paris.
White, J. H., Collins Street West.
Conrad, Captain, ship "Herzog Ernst."
Grant, Charles Lyall, Shanghai.

Stackpool, Captain, ship "Shannon."
Cooper, Captain, ship "Carlisle Castle."
Consul for Austria.
" " Belgium.
" " Brazil.
" " Chili.
" " Denmark.
" " France.
" " German Empire.

Consul for Hawaii.
" " Italy.
" " Netherlands.
" " Peru.
" " Portugal.
" " Russia.
" " Spain.
" " Sweden and Norway.
" " United States.

SUPPLEMENTAL LIST OF MEMBERS,

To 15th May, 1874.

Name	£	s	d
Anderson & Wright, Flinders-lane	1	1	0
Amess, Samuel, William-street	1	1	0
Ayrey, C., Warranuke	10	10	0
Black, Dr. J., Bourke-street	2	2	0
Banks, Bros., Bell & Co., Flinders-lane	2	2	0
Briscoe and Co., Collins-street	2	2	0
Barnes, W., Brunswick	1	1	0
Baines, E., Little Collins-street	2	2	0
Bindon, Judge, St. Kilda	1	1	0
Bligh and Harbottle, Flinders-lane	2	2	0
Curtain, J., M.L.A., Elgin.street	2	2	0
Crosby, W., Queen-street	1	1	0
Crooke, Dr., Gertrude-street	1	1	0
Cornwall, A., Brunswick	1	1	0
Dempster, A., Royal Park	1	1	0
Elkington, J., Educational Office	1	1	0
Edwards, Henry, Bourke-street	1	1	0
Evans, Gowen, "Argus" office	2	2	0
Fanning, Nankivell and Co., Flinders-street	2	2	0
Frew, G., Royal Park	1	1	0
Finlay, John, Emerald Hill	1	1	0
Foy, Mark, Smith-street	1	1	0
Fynn, John, Kilmore	1	1	0
Fox, W., Tallarook	1	1	0
Fergusson and Moore, Flinders-lane	1	1	0
Fleetwood, T. P., Chancery-lane	1	1	0
Goldsbrough, R., and Co., Bourke-street	2	2	0
Grice, R., Flinders-lane	1	1	0
Gibson, R., Royal Park	2	2	0
Glew, John, Brunswick	1	1	0
Heath, R. M., Kilmore	1	1	0
Hunt, Thos., M.L.A., Kilmore	1	1	0
Hoddle, R. Bourke-street	2	0	0
Hay, William, Boomanoomana	10	10	0
Inglis, D., Flinders-street	1	1	0
James, J. R., Royal Park	1	1	0
Jacobs, F., and Co., Queen-street	1	1	0
Larnach, J. m. D., Kilmore	1	1	0
Lobb, W. J., M.L.A., Brunswick	1	1	0
Laing and Webster, Flinders-lane	1	1	0
Long, D. R., Bourke-street	1	1	0
Manallack, Thos., Brunswick	1	1	0
McIlwraith, J., Little Collins-street	1	1	0
McNaughton, Love & Co., Flinders-lane	1	1	0
Murphy, E. J., William-street	1	1	0
Martin, George, Market-street	2	2	0
Malloson and England, Queen-st.	1	1	0
Martin, P. J., Flinders-lane	1	1	0
Matheson, J., Collins-street	1	1	0
McDougall, C., Brunswick	1	1	0
Martin, T., Brunswick	1	1	0
McCoy, Professor, University	1	1	0
O'Connor, J. D., Kilmore	1	1	0
Officer, C. M., Brighton	2	2	0
Osborne, James, Merton Lodge, Elsternwick	1	1	0
Overend, Best, Brunswick	2	2	0
Perry, John, Lonsdale-street	1	1	0
Peterson, W. and Co., Queen-street	1	1	0
Paterson, Ray, Palmer and Co., Flinders-lane	2	2	0
Ryan and Hammond, Bourke-st.	2	2	0
Rowe and Stodart, Miller's Ponds	2	2	0
Rocke, W. H. Collins-street	1	1	0
Russell, Hon. P., M.L.C., Brighton road	10	10	0
Rosser, Mrs. Charles, Brunswick	1	1	0
Ritchie, J., Streatham	10	0	0
Sprigg, W. G., Market-street	1	1	0
Stevenson and Elliott, Lonsdale-st.	1	1	0

DONATIONS.

	£ s d		£ s d
Simson, John, Waverly, Kew	£1 1 0	Taylor, W., Keilor	£2 2 0
Swallow and Ariel, Sandridge	1 1 0	Taylor, T. H., Chancery-lane	1 1 0
Sloane, W., and Co., Collins-street	1 1 0	Twentyman, R., Flinders-street	1 1 0
Sprigg, G., St. Kilda	1 1 0	Vetter, John, Echuca	1 1 0
Smith, C. and J., Albert-street	1 1 0	Wilson, Henry, Kilmore	1 1 0
Sargood, Son and Co., Flinders-st	2 2 0	Watson, George, Burnet-street, St. Kilda	1 1 0
Sands and McDougall, Collins-street	2 2 0	Wilson, Edward, "Argus" office	2 2 0
Sanderson, J., and Co., William-st.	1 1 0	Welch, Henry P., Queen-street	1 1 0
Stanford and Co., Bourke street	1 1 0	Wood, J., and Son, Wellington-street, Collingwood	1 1 0
Strong, Professor, University	1 1 0	Wilshin and Leighton, William-st.	1 1 0
Taylor, J., Kilmore	1 1 0		
Tinning, J., Brunswick	1 1 0		
Terry, A., Royal Park	1 1 0		

THE RULES AND OBJECTS

OF THE

Zoological & Acclimatisation Society

OF VICTORIA.

Objects of Society.

1. The objects of the Society shall be the introduction, acclimatisation, liberation, and domestication of innoxious animals and vegetables, whether useful or ornamental;—the perfection, propagation, and hybridisation of races newly introduced, or already domesticated;—the spread of indigenous animals, &c., from parts of the colonies where they are already known, to other localities where they are not known;—the procuring, whether by purchase, gift, or exchange, of animals, &c.;—the transmission of animals, &c., from the colony to England and foreign parts, in exchange for, others sent thence to the Society;—the collection and maintenance of zoological specimens, for exhibition or otherwise;—the holding of periodical meetings, and the publication of reports and transactions, for the purpose of spreading knowledge of acclimatisation, and inquiry into the causes of success or failure;—the interchange of reports, &c., with kindred associations in other parts of the world, with the view, by correspondence and mutual good offices, of giving the widest possible scope to the project of acclimatisation;—the conferring rewards, honorary or intrinsically valuable, upon persons who may render valuable services to the cause of acclimatisation.

Membership.

2. A Subscriber of one guinea or upwards annually, which shall be payable in the month of January, shall be a

Member of the Society; and contributors, within one year, of ten guineas or upwards shall be Life Members of the Society; and any person who may render special services to the Society, by contribution of stock or otherwise, shall be eligible for life membership, and may be elected as such by the Council, or by any annual general meeting.

3. All the property of the Society shall vest in the Council for the time being, for the use, purposes, and benefit of the Society. *Property vest in the Council.*

4. The Society shall be governed by a Council of twelve Members, to include a President, two Vice-Presidents, and an Honorary Treasurer, who shall annually retire from office, and three other Members (viz., those who have attended the fewest Meetings of the Council proportionately since their appointment) shall also retire annually, but shall be eligible for re-election, subject to Rule 13. Provided that if any sum of money be voted to the Society by Act of Parliament, or trusts conferred upon the Council by the Government, then it shall be lawful for the Chief Secretary for the time being to appoint, if he consider it expedient, any number of gentlemen, not exceeding three, to act as Members of the Council, and they shall have all the privileges as if otherwise duly elected. *Executive Officers. Council.*

5. In case of a vacancy occurring by the death, resignation, or non-attendance of any Member of the Council for a period of two months, without leave of the Council, the remaining Members shall, in due course, appoint another Member of the Society to be a Member of the Council in the place and stead of the Member who shall so resign or absent himself; but such new Member shall be nominated at an ordinary meeting of the Council prior to the meeting at which he is elected. *Vacancy in Council, how supplied.*

6. In case of a vacancy occurring by the death or resignation of the President, Vice-President, or Hon. Treasurer, the Council may appoint from amongst themselves, or the other Members of the Society, a person to fill the vacancy so occurring, and the person elected shall hold office only until the next Annual Meeting; but shall be eligible for re-election *Council to fill up Vacancies.*

for the subsequent year. Provided that such vacancy shall not be filled up unless seven days' notice in writing shall have been sent to each Member of the Council, stating the vacancies which it is proposed to fill up.

Eligibility of Members of Council
7. No person shall be eligible as a Member of Council unless he be a subscriber to the funds of the Society of at least one guinea per annum; and any Member of Council whose subscription shall be in arrear for three months after his subscription is payable, shall cease to be a Member of Council: Provided that this rule shall not apply to persons who may have become Life Members of the Society, by a payment of ten guineas, or who may be Honorary Members of the Society; and provided also, that a month's notice in writing shall be sent to the Member before his place can be filled up.

Meetings of Council.
8. The Council shall meet at least once a month, three Members to form a quorum, and transact the business of the Society.

Powers and Duties of Council.
9. The Council shall have the sole management of the affairs of the Society, and of the income and property thereof, for the uses, purposes, and benefit of the Society; and shall have the sole and exclusive right of appointing paid servants, as a Manager or Secretary, Collector, and such other officers, clerks, and labourers, and at such salaries as they may deem necessary, and of removing them if they shall think fit, and shall prescribe their respective duties. And such Council shall have power to consider and determine all matters, either directly or indirectly affecting the interests of the Society, and if they shall think fit so to do, shall bring the same under the notice of the Members of the Society, at any general or special meeting; and to make such bye-laws as they may deem necessary for the efficient management of the affairs and the promotion of the objects of the Society, and for the conduct of the business of the Council: Provided the same are not repugnant to these rules; to appoint one or more sub-committees, for any purpose contemplated by these rules; and

generally to perform such acts as may be requisite to carry out the objects of the Society.

10. The Society shall have power to associate itself with other Societies with similar objects, and to found Branch Societies. Branch Societies, &c.

11. Minutes shall be made, in books kept for the purpose, of all proceedings at general and special meetings of the Members, and minutes shall also be made of the proceedings of the Council at their general and special meetings, and of the names of the Members attending the same, and such minutes shall be open to inspection by any Member of the Society at all reasonable times. Minutes of Proceedings.

12. All subscriptions and other moneys received on account of the Society shall be paid to the Treasurer, or some person authorised by him in writing, who shall forthwith place the same in a bank, to be named by the Council, to the credit of the Society; and no sum shall be paid on account of the Society until the same shall have been ordered by the Council, and such order be duly entered in the book of the proceedings of the Council; and all cheques shall be signed by the Treasurer as such, and be countersigned by the President, or one of the Vice-Presidents, or by the Chairman of the meeting at which such payment is authorised. Moneys to be paid to Treasurer.

13. An annual meeting shall be held in the month of February of each year, and the Council shall report their proceedings during the past year, and shall produce their accounts, duly audited, for publication; and the meeting shall elect by ballot the office-bearers for the ensuing year, and fill up any vacancy which may exist in the Council: Provided that no person shall hold the office of President or Vice-President, for two years successively. Annual Meeting

14. The Council may, and upon receiving a requisition in writing, signed by twelve or more Members, shall convene a special meeting of the Members, to be held within fifteen days after the receipt of such requisition: Provided that such requisition, and the notices convening the meeting, shall Special Meetings of Members

specify the subject to be considered at such meeting, and that such subject only shall be discussed at such meeting.

Honorary Members. 15. The Council, or any general meeting of the Society, may admit, as Honorary Members, any ladies or gentlemen who may have distinguished themselves in connexion with the objects of the Society, and at such meeting any other business of the Society shall be transacted, of which one day's previous notice shall have been given to the Secretary by any Member desirous of bringing the same forward.

16. No Medal of the Society shall be awarded to any person except by the vote of at least seven Members of Council present at a Council Meeting, and after notice of motion for awarding such Medal shall have been given at the next preceding meeting of the Council.

Power to alter Rules. 17. It shall be lawful for any annual or special meeting of the Society to alter, vary, or amend the rules ; or to substitute another for any of the same ; or to make any new rule which may be considered desirable ; if and after a notice specifying the nature of such alteration, variation, amendment, substitution, or new rule, shall have been given to the Secretary fifteen days before the holding of such meeting. And such alteration, variation, amendment, substitution, or new rule shall be valid if carried by a majority of not less than two-thirds of the Members present at such meeting.

LIST OF ANIMALS AND BIRDS

IN THE ZOOLOGICAL GARDENS, ROYAL PARK.

ANIMALS.

1 African Lion } *Felis Leo.*
1 African Lioness }
1 Hunting Leopard—*Felis Jubata.*
1 Panther or Leopard—*Leopardus Varius.*
1 Silver Jackall—*Canis Mesomelas.*
2 Native Dogs.—*Canis Dingo.*
1 Marsupial Wolf—*Thylacinus Cynocephalus.*
1 Tasmanian Devil—*Sarcophilus Ursinus.*
4 Native Cats—*Dasyurus Viverrinus.*
1 Tiger Cat—*Dasyurus Maculatus.*
1 Moongus—*Herpestes Griseus.*
1 Beelbah—*Paragalea Lagotis.*
2 American Black Bears—*Ursus Americanus.*
2 Chacmas, or Ursine Baboons—*Cynocephalus Porcarius.*
15 Monkeys of different varieties.
1 Native Bear—*Phascolarctus Cinereus.*
1 Wombat—*Phascolmys Platyrhinus.*

1 Wombat—*Lasyorhinus McCoyi.*
3 Red Kangaroos—*Osphranter Rufus.*
4 Large Kangaroos—*Macropus Major.*
1 Bennett's Kangaroo—*Halmaturus Bennetti.*
5 Yellow footed Rock Wallabys—*Petrogale Xanthopus.*
2 Gloved Wallaby—*Halmaturus Manicatus.*
1 Black Wallaby—*Halmaturus Ualabutus.*
4 Kangaroo rats—*Bettongia Cuniculus.*
3 Opossums—*Phalangista Valpino.*
42 Deer of different varieties.
4 Sheep of different varieties.
5 Brahmin cattle.
45 Angora goats.

156

BIRDS.

26 English Pheasants—*Phasianus Colchicus.*
8 Golden Pheasants—*Chrysolophus Pictus.*
15 Japanese Green Pheasants—*Phasianus Versicolor.*
1 Reeves's Pheasant—*Syrmaticus Reeves.*
8 Silver Pheasants—*Phasianus Nycthemerus.*
5 Emus—*Dromaius Novæ Hollandiæ.*
3 Native Companions—*Grus Australasianus.*
1 White Crane—*Herodias Syrmatophorus.*
1 Black-backed Water Hen—*Parphyrio Melanotus.*
1 Nankeen Night Heron—*Nysticorax Caledonicus.*
1 Kagu—*Rhinochætus Jubatus.*
2 White Swans—*Cygnus Olor.*
2 White Swans—*Cygnus Buccinator.*
2 Black Swans—*Cygnus Atratus.*
4 Cape Barren Geese—*Cereopsis Novæ Hollandiæ.*
2 Bar-headed Geese—*Anser Indicus.*
3 Egyptian Geese—*Chenalopex Ægyptiaca.*
3 Magpie Geese—*Anseranas Melanoleuca.*
4 Paradise Ducks—*Casarca Variegata.*
5 Mandarin Ducks—*Aix Galericulata.*
50 Ducks of different varieties.
5 Australian Eagles—*Aquila Andax.*
4 Hawks of different varieties.
1 Owl—*Bubo Bengalensis.*
1 Owl—*Strix Custanops.*
3 Ravens—*Corvus Corax.*

2 Laughing Jackasses—*Dacelo Gigas.*
4 Macaws—*Ara Araganza.*
40 Parrots, different varieties.
17 Cockatoos of different varieties.
1 Crowned Pigeon—*Goura Coronata.*
2 Wonga Wonga Pigeons—*Leucosarcia Picata.*
7 Bleeding Heart Pigeons—*Calœnas Luzonica.*
20 Doves of various sorts.
2 Curassows—*Crax Alector.*
8 Blackbirds—*Turdus Merula.*
44 Canaries—*Carduelis Canaria.*
4 Satin Bower Birds—*Ptilonorhynchus Holosericeus.*
3 White Stone Plovers—*Ædicnemus Grallarius.*
1 Native Turkey—*Otis Australasianus.*
1 Australian Magpie—*Gymnorhina Leuconota.*
1 Maori Hen, the Weka rail—*Ocydromus Australis.*
1 Malee Hen or Lowan—*Leipoa Ocellata.*
1 Red Legged Partridge—*Caccabis Rufa.*
4 English Partridges—*Perdix Cinereus.*
4 Californian Quail—*Callipepla Californica.*
2 Pea Fowl—*Pavo Christatus.*

329

AT MR. SAMUEL WILSON'S ESTATE, ERCILDOUN.

140 Angora goats.

The Ostriches have been removed to Mr. Officer's Station, Murray Downs.

LIST OF DONORS TO THE ZOOLOGICAL AND ACCLIMATISATION SOCIETY, 1873-4.

AMESS, MR.—2 Laughing Jackasses, 3 Black Swans.
ATKIN, C. A., HOTHAM.—2 Iguanas, 2 Freshwater Turtle, 2 Quail.
BROWNLESS, DR.—1 Bandicoot.
BALLARAT FISH ACCLIMATISATION SOCIETY.—22 English Perch.
BALLARAT, MUNICIPAL COUNCIL OF.—1 Pair White Swans.
BENBOW, MR., RUSHWORTH.—2 Kangaroos.
BELL, ALFRED, BOURKE STREET.—1 Wallaby, 1 White Hawk.
BOTANIC GARDENS, FROM.—2 Monkeys, 1 Kangaroo Rat, 1 Emu, 1 Native Companion.
BATHE, DR. DANDENONG.—1 Dingo.
CARSON, MISS MARIAN.—1 Kangaroo.
CLARKE, J. W.—1 brace Hares.
CAMPBELL, J. GLENCOE.—2 Black Swans.
CHIRNSIDE, MESSRS.—1 Dingo.
ELLIOTT, GEORGE, DENILIQUIN.—5 Kangaroos.
FORD, MR., TOWN CLERK OF SANDHURST.—1 Eagle.
GINGELL, MR., BAIRNSDALE—1 Hawk.
GODFREY, F. R., MOUNT RIDLEY—1 Plover, 1 Large Lizard.
GASKIN, MR., TEMPLE COURT.—2 Moloch Lizards.
GIBBS, MASTER HENRY, GLENVALE.—1 Kangaroo.
GRANT, CHARLES LYALL, SHANGHAE.—8 Golden Pheasants, 1 Reeves Pheasant.
HENDY, MR., MERRIANG.—1 Eagle, 1 Mopoke.
HICKFORD, MR., BRUNSWICK.—1 Stone Plover.
HAINES, MRS.—1 Fallow Deer.
HENTY, MR., MUNTHAM.—2 Kestrils.
JONES, LLOYD, AVENEL.—1 Porcupine Anteater.
JEMMETT, G., SHIP Shannon.—8 Blackbirds.
KISSLEY, GEORGE, NIMAR.—4 Kangaroos, 1 Native Companion, 1 Black Swan, 16 Magpie Geese, 1 pair White Cranes, 4 Mopokes, 1 Plover.
MILLER, CAPTAIN, SHIP Suffolk.—1 Raven.
MURRAY, MR., PINJARRAH, WEST AUSTRALIA.—1 Black Cockatoo.
MINNETT, MR.—1 Porcupine Ant Eater.
METTERS, JAMES, LONSDALE-STREET.—1 Monkey.
MESSETER, MR. RICHMOND.—1 Kangaroo.
MOLESWORTH, ROBERT.—1 Mallee Hen or Lowan.
MOODY, LESLIE, SOUTH YARRA.—1 Monkey.
MCEACHERN, D., HOTSPUR.—2 Emus.
OFFICER, S. H., MURRAY DOWNS—2 Emus, 1 Kangaroo.
OFFICER, C. M., BRIGHTON.—1 Native Companion.
OLIVER, MR., COLIBAN PARK.—2 Kangaroo Rats.
OGILVIE, CHARLES, PORT AUGUSTA.—20 Moloch Lizards.
PURCHAS, ALBERT, KEW.—1 pair Pheasants.
PURVES, MR., WEST MELBOURNE.—1 Iguana.
RADDENBERRY, J.—2 Porcupine Ant Eaters.
SCOTT, ROBERT, MURRUMBIDGEE.—4 English Partridges.
STAUGHTON, MR., EXFORD.—1 Kangaroo.
SHANN, MR., BANK OF VICTORIA.—1 Dingo.
SCHOMBURGK, DR., ADELAIDE.—1 Port Lincoln Wombat, 1 Ibis, 1 Deer.
SPENCE, MR.—1 Porcupine Ant Eater.
SUMNER, HON. T. J., STONEY PARK.—1 Silver Pheasant.

STOCK SOLD, &c.

TERRY, MISS, ROYAL PARK.—1 Kangaroo Rat.
TURNER, MR., TOORAK.—1 Platypus.
WALL, MR., EMERALD HILL—1 Kangaroo.
WORTHINGTON, MR., AVENEL.—1 Emu.
WEIR, MR., STRATFORD.—4 Black Swans.
WARE, MASTER G. J. W.—1 Flying Squirrel.
ZOOLOGICAL SOCIETY OF LONDON.—2 Macaws, 1 pair Trumpeter Swans, 1 pair Ducks.

STOCK ACQUIRED DURING THE YEAR 1873-4, BY PURCHASE OR EXCHANGE.

3 Angora Goats—exchange.
1 American Black Bear—exchange.
4 Black tailed Parrakeets—purchase.
32 Canaries—purchase.
40 Californian Quail—exchange.
2 Chacma or Ursine Baboons—exchange.
9 Cockatoos—purchase.
8 Mandarin Ducks—exchange.
4 Magpie Geese—purchase.
10 Parrots—purchase.
1 Platypus—purchase.
1 Satin Bower Bird—purchase.
1 Tasmanian Marsupial Wolf—purchase.

STOCK SOLD, PRESENTED, OR EXCHANGED, BY THE SOCIETY DURING THE YEAR 1873-4.

4 Angora Goats—exchange.
2 do. do. presented to the Western Australian Government.
5 do. do. sold.
2 do. do. presented to Mr. Kissley of the Nimar.
4 Black Swans—presented to James McLachlan, Esq.
6 do. do. exchange.
4 do. do. presented to Captain Bailley, of Galle.
1 Cape Barren Goose—presented to Professor McCoy.
8 Cockatoos—exchange.
1 Dingo—exchange.
8 Emus—presented to Captain Cooper, ship *Carlisle Castle*.
2 do. presented to the Hon. J. J. Casey and Sir Charles G. Duffy for the Zoological Society of Dublin.
2 Emus—presented to James McLachlan, Esq.
2 do. presented to Charles Lyall Grant, Esq., Shanghae.
8 Egyptian Geese—presented to the Municipal Council of Ballarat.
2 Eagles—presented to the Hon. J. J. Casey and Sir Charles G. Duffy, for the Zoological Society of Dublin.
4 Hares—exchange.
7 do. presented to the West Australian Government.
2 Hog Deer—presented to Mr. Gill of Seymour.
4 Indian Black Duck—presented to the Municipal Council of Ballarat.
6 Kangaroos—exchange.
2 do. presented to Charles Lyall Grant, Esq., Shanghae.
2 do. presented to the Zoological Society of London.
1 do. presented to Captain Cooper, ship *Carlisle Castle*.
4 Kangaroo Rats—exchange.
16 Magpie Geese—exchange.
2 New Zealand Paradise Ducks—presented to the Municipal Council of Ballarat.
2 do. do. exchange.
3 Native Companions—exchange.
2 White Swans—presented to the Municipal Council of Sandhurst.
1 Tasmanian Devil—exchange.

In addition to the above a number of male Angora Goats were sold by Mr. S. Wilson.

ANIMALS LIBERATED.

ANIMALS LIBERATED PREVIOUS TO 1870.

AT THE BOTANICAL GARDENS.

18 Canaries	6 California quail	4 English robins
18 Blackbirds	80 English wild ducks	8 Turtle doves
14 Thrushes	35 Java sparrows	50 Mainas

AT PHILLIP ISLAND.

10 Hares	70 Chinese quail	6 Skylarks
22 Pheasants	23 Tasmanian quail	6 California quail
8 Ceylon partridges	6 Starlings	4 Thrushes
5 Indian partridges	10 Algerine sand grouse	4 Blackbirds
4 Chinese partridges	6 Wild ducks	1 Pair white swans

AT SANDSTONE AND CHURCHILL ISLANDS.

4 Pheasants	4 Skylarks	4 Thrushes

AT YARRA BEND.

6 Thrushes	4 Skylarks

NEAR SYDNEY.

9 Thrushes	4 Skylarks	10 Blackbirds

AT SUGARLOAF HILL.

5 Ceylon elk	3 Axis deer

AT WILSON'S PROMONTORY.

4 Axis deer

AT THE ROYAL PARK.

4 Hares	2 Thrushes	20 Siskin finches
20 Mainas	20 Greenfinches	6 Powi birds
6 Starlings	15 Yellowhammers	3 Partridges
60 English sparrows	200 Java sparrows	6 Pheasants
40 Chaffinches	6 Blackbirds	10 English robins

AT BALLARAT.

5 English sparrows	20 Java sparrows	4 Indian black duck
2 Paradise ducks	2 Egyptian geese	

AT DUNEEP.

13 Fallow deer

AT CAPE LIPTRAP.

12 Hog deer	4 Ceylon peafowls	4 Guinea fowl
	10 Pigeons	

AT AUCKLAND ISLANDS.

12 Goats	12 Rabbits	6 Fowls
3 Geese	3 Pigs	3 Ducks

ANIMALS LIBERATED.

AT WESTERNPORT.
7 Sambur deer

AT THE WIMMERA.
35 Axis deer

AT YERING.
5 Axis deer

AT PLENTY RANGES.
10 Pheasants. | 4 Jungle fowls. | 7 Guinea fowls.

LIBERATED IN THE BUSH IN 1870.

8 Hog deer	30 Pheasants	A number of doves
10 Pea fowl	Several brace of hares	25 Skylarks
20 Guinea fowl		

A large number of hares were likewise distributed in 1870 in various parts of the country, and upwards of 100 Angora goats were disposed of.

LIBERATED IN THE BUSH IN 1871.

| 150 Guinea fowl | Several brace of hares |
| 15 Pheasants | 3 Deer |

And 2,400 trout fry placed in different streams.
A number of hares were likewise distributed in various parts of the country.

LIBERATED IN THE BUSH IN 1872.

| 50 Pheasants | 17 English robins |
| 20 Guinea fowl | A number of Californian quail. |

1,700 carp, a number of English perch, and several hundred trout fry placed in suitable streams and reservoirs.
In addition to the above, 54 pheasants have been sold and distributed to Members of the Society.

LIBERATED IN THE BUSH IN 1873-4.

100 Pheasants	9 Pea fowl	16 Doves
100 Skylarks	30 Hares	12 Guinea fowl
40 Californian quail	5 Deer	9 French Partridges

More than 2000 Carp and a number of English Perch have likewise been distributed, also about 800 Brown Trout.
200 Pheasant Eggs were likewise distributed to members of the Society.

D

ANIMALS SENT AWAY.

TO LONDON.

85 Kangaroos	30 Waterhens	40 Black ducks
5 Mountain ducks	4 Kangaroo rats	40 Teal
200 Murray codfish	10 Wombats	22 Wonga pigeons
32 Black swans	2 Cranes	31 Bronze-wing pigeons
20 Australian quail	7 Wood ducks	8 Swamp magpies
14 Eagle hawks	2 Kangaroo dogs	2 Iguanas
85 Magpies	3 Echidna	7 Land rails
4 Rosella parrots	26 Laughing jackasses	4 Sugar squirrels
8 King parrots	40 Shell parrots	3 Coots
16 Cockatoos	6 Mallee pheasants	5 Native companions
5 Dingos	36 Lowry parrots	Some Yarra fish
3 Talegallas	12 Opossums	16 Magpie geese
1 Tasmanian devil	9 Emus	

TO DUBLIN.

2 Eagles		2 Emus

TO PARIS.

24 Emus	3 Curlews	8 Goatsuckers
30 Kangaroos	1 Native crane	2 Native companions
12 Black swans	8 Murray turtles	14 Rockhampton finches
3 Cape Barren geese	2 Wombats	1 Iguana
1 South Australian wombat	17 Australian quail	4 Opossums
4 Native geese	4 Laughing jackasses	20 Black ducks
	2 Bronze-wing pigeons	20 Teal

TO ST. PETERSBURG.

3 Kangaroos	2 Laughing jackasses	3 Emus
3 Black swans	2 Wallabies	

TO AMSTERDAM.

3 Water hens		6 Australian quail

TO ROTTERDAM.

2 Cape Barren geese	2 Water hens	2 Kangaroos

TO HAMBURGH.

2 Wonga pigeons	2 Bronze-wing pigeons	2 Kangaroo rats
2 Black swans		

TO PHILADELPHIA.

3 Native Companions	3 Magpie Geese	4 Kangaroo rats
2 Paradise ducks	1 Wild dog	2 Kangaroos

TO COLOGNE.

2 Black swans	2 Curlews	2 Water hens
2 Magpie geese		

ANIMALS SENT AWAY.

TO COPENHAGEN.
2 Black swans

TO CALCUTTA.

24 Black swans	15 Rosella parrots	6 Bronze-wing pigeons
12 Emus	10 Kangaroos	6 Laughing jackasses
2 Eagles	4 Opossums	20 Shell parrots
6 White cockatoos	1 Dingo	52 Magpies
7 King parrots	1 Wombat	

TO MAURITIUS.

2 Black swans	2 Eagle hawks	2 Laughing jackasses
1 Kangaroo	9 Fowls	4 Wallabies
2 Cape Barren geese	7 Magpies	

TO BOURBON.
8 Black swans

TO SICILY.

6 Black swans	14 Native ducks

TO RANGOON.
6 Black Swans

TO JAVA.

2 Black swans	2 Cape Barren geese	1 Kangaroo

TO BURTENZONG.

2 Black swans	2 Cape Barren geese	1 Kangaroo

TO SYDNEY.

6 Angora goats	2 Egyptian geese	10 Thrushes
2 Brush kangaroos	6 English wild ducks	4 Larks
2 Silver pheasants	1 Mallee hen	4 Starlings
2 Canadian geese	10 Blackbirds	2 Ortolans

TO ADELAIDE.

13 Angora goats	2 Thrushes	1 Fallow deer
2 Blackbirds	3 English pheasants	7 Silver pheasants
1 Brahmin Bull		

TO WEST AUSTRALIA.

4 Angora gaots	7 Hares	2 Deer

ANIMALS SENT AWAY.

TO HOBART TOWN.

3 Angora goats
9 Native bears
Wild ducks, Indian & English

4 Egyptian geese
4 Hares

TO NEW ZEALAND.

3 Thrushes
6 Magpies

4 Opossums
10 Brace of hares

Indian and English wild ducks

TO FOO CHOW.

48 Wild rabbits | 2 Kangaroo | 2 Parrots

TO NEW CALEDONIA.

238 Sparrows | 12 Laughing jackasses

TO SHANGHAI.

2 Kangaroos.

TO YOKOHAMA.

2 Emus | 2 Kangaroos

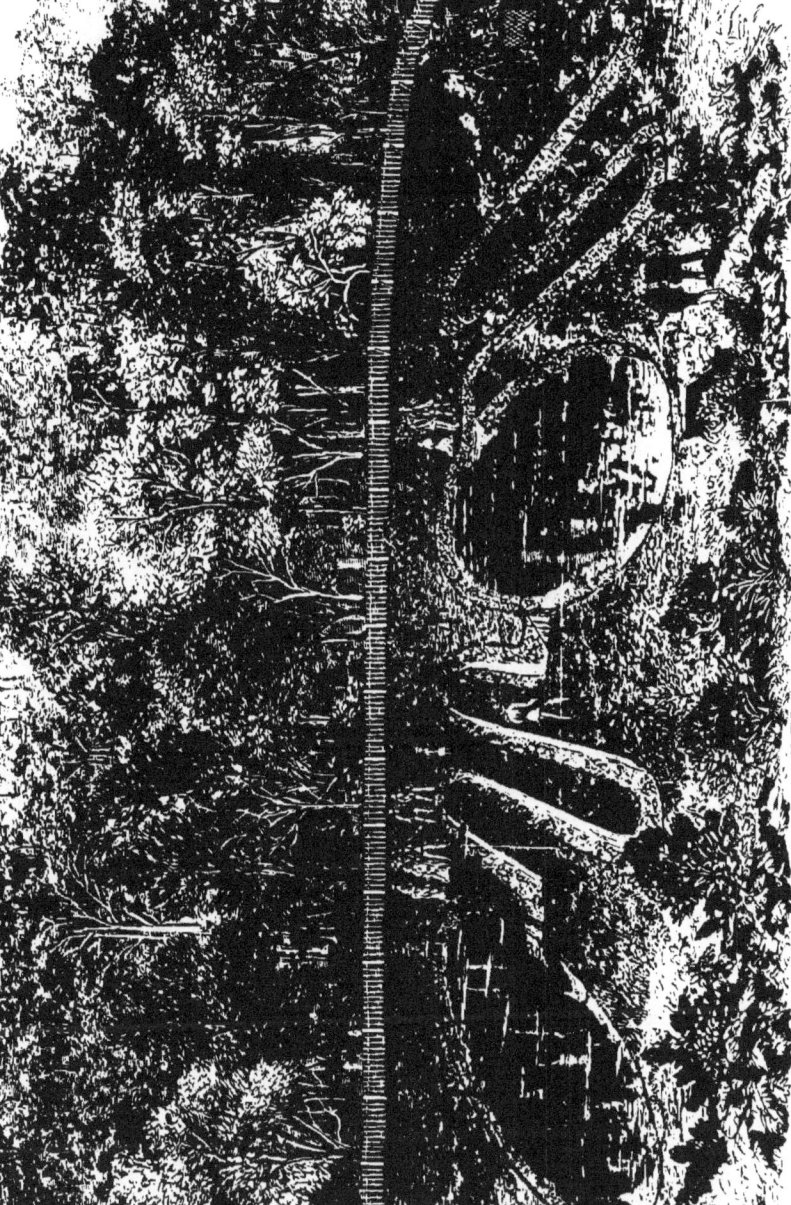

A REPORT
ON THE
FISH BREEDING PONDS
OF THE
ZOOLOGICAL AND ACCLIMATISATION SOCIETY
OF VICTORIA,

AND

INTRODUCTION OF FISH INTO THE RIVERS OF
THE COLONY.

By CURZON ALLPORT.

The following are extracts from a description of the ponds which appeared in the *Australasian Sketcher* in April last, the frontispiece to this report being, by permission of the proprietors, taken from the illustration in that paper :—

"The ponds are upon the private property of Mr. William Robertson, at Wooling, near Gisborne, about 40 miles from Melbourne. An area has been enclosed of about two acres of land, prettily situated upon a stream which takes its rise in the neighbouring spurs of Mount Macedon. A water race, supplied from this stream for Mr. Robertson's saw-mill, takes in its course a bend away from the stream, approaching it again at a lower point, and an oval space is thus formed, which, after falling a few feet from the level of the race, continues almost a flat to the bank of the stream, which here runs a cold, clear, fern-hidden brook, some 15ft. or 20ft. below. This space, which is above all danger from floods, has been cleared and planted with English grasses, and in its centre are the ponds.

There are two ponds, each being about 70ft. long by 40ft. in width, and shelving to a depth of about 5ft. in the deepest part; they are pitched with rough stone, artificial caves or hides being made for the fish. Above each pond there is what is termed a rill, along which water flows before entering the respective ponds. These rills are about 4ft. wide at the lower end, where they enter the ponds, and about 8in. or 9in. deep, shoaling gradually to 2in. or 3in. at the upper end; they are serpentine in form to give greater length, being about 66 yards long. Into the upper one water is admitted from the mill race, and this flows through the whole length of rills, and through the ponds. The ponds are also supplied directly from the race. The upper race and ponds are tenanted at present by some 200 or 300 brown trout, which were hatched in October last from ova obtained from Tasmania, while the lower pond is occupied by English salmon trout, hatched at the same time from ova similarly obtained. It is intended to keep 25 or 30 parent fish in each of the ponds, leaving them to deposit their ova naturally in the rills which are made for the purpose, means being taken to prevent the access of large fish from the ponds after the ova have been deposited; ova and young fish will afterwards be distributed throughout the colony to stock suitable streams."

Owing to the great attention which Tasmania has absorbed, and deservedly so, in fish acclimatisation in Australasia, comparatively little is known of what has been done in Victoria, but real and substantial progress has nevertheless been made, notwithstanding that there have been mistakes and much delay, while those who have been doing the work have been content to do it quietly and unknown, in order that they should be less interfered with and their endeavours should succeed.

Victorian rivers are not, so far as the writer is aware, adapted for salmon, and, unlike Tasmania, comparatively few are adapted for salmon trout,

FISH BREEDING PONDS. 39

but for the brown or English trout its streams have been proved to be well adapted, and when our ponds have reached the age of those in Tasmania, and Victoria has made up the valuable time which has been lost, results equal, if not superior, to those in the sister colony should be seen.

When the first salmon and trout ova arrived from England *en route* to Tasmania, in April, 1862, three boxes of salmon ova were retained, as a safeguard and experiment. The ova were hatched at the Victoria Ice Company's Works, under the care of the then Secretary of the Society, and the fry were placed by Mr. Ramsbottom in the Badger Creek, a tributary of the Upper Yarra, since when nothing authentic is known of them. The gentleman in whose charge they were placed prior to their being turned out, and who has been a salmon fisher in Scotland, declares that he has since heard salmon leaping in that tributary. Would he were right!

Of salmon trout more will be said presently in connection with the ponds. The books of the Society show that in 1863, in remitting monies to England towards the expense of a second shipment of salmon ova, instructions were given to Mr. Youl to send salmon trout ova also.

The trout ova which arrived on the occasion referred to were procured by Mr. Frank Buckland and Mr. Francis Francis from the best trout streams in England, for Mr. Youl, and were sent by him as a present to Mr. Edward Wilson, in this colony, who, at Mr. Ramsbottom's earnest request, very wisely allowed them to go to Tasmania, proper appliances being ready there to receive and hatch them—it being promised that Victoria should receive a fair share of the produce; a promise which has been faithfully and amply performed.

From the ova thus sent to Tasmania about 300 young fish were obtained, and these formed the total stock of English trout there.

The first ova and young fish received from Tasmania were lost—the ova, with the apparatus in which they were placed, near Sunbury, being carried away by an unusually high flood; the young fish were lost owing to their care and management not being understood. The next supply of young fish were turned out, and have bred. With the later supplies, more especially during the last few years, better progress has been made; but, no doubt, little has been done compared to what would have been the result had breeding ponds been constructed, as they should have been, at first.

The supplies from Tasmania were distributed on arrival, either to local societies or to private individuals, or, in the case of young fish, direct into suitable streams, but each year, until the last, when the ponds were constructed, ova were retained by the Society and hatched at the Society's gardens, in the Royal Park, at Melbourne, in a house and apparatus built for that purpose and supplied with water from the Yan Yean reservoir. The experience gained by this course was useful, but the result not always satisfactory; one year the per centage of loss would not exceed 20, but in others there would scarcely be more than that per centage saved. This was attributable to the uncertain water supply, the distance the water had to travel through pipes, and the occasional rise in temperature.

FISH BREEDING PONDS.

These reasons, and the distance from suitable streams, made the Council of the Society abandon hatching at the gardens.

The increasing demand from all parts of Southern Australia and New Zealand upon Tasmania for ova and fish, and its own requirements, necessarily prevented an annual supply being continued; and therefore it became necessary, if Victorian streams were to be stocked, that breeding ponds should be established in the colony.

Mention may appropriately be here made before mentioning the ponds, of the success which has already been achieved with the supplies referred to. Young fish have been placed by the Society in the Watts' River and other headwaters of the Yarra; in Riddle's Creek, and other streams which empty themselves into the Deep Creek and Saltwater River; in the head waters of the Coliban, which flows northwards to the Murray; in the head waters of the Broken River, which take their rise in the north-eastern division of the colony; at Kilmore, in the same division; in Darlott's Creek, in the western division; in waters near Stawell, in the north-western division; and in streams taking their rise in the Dandenong Ranges to the south; and also in the Yan Yean Reservoir.

The above is independent of the distribution by local societies, and in speaking of their success special mention is to be made of the society at Ballarat, which will probably next year distribute ova from its ponds. It successfully hatched trout during the seasons 1871-2-3. The young fish were distributed into more than twenty streams of the western district, and those turned out in 1871 have without doubt multiplied during 1873.

The streams of the colony have not yet been thrown open for trout fishing, and therefore but few instances can be given of the success of the fish turned out. While lowering the water recently in the race which supplies the Society's ponds, more than a dozen young fish were seen, weighing from half a pound downwards; these are the produce of fish turned into the stream about four years ago. Near Ballan a trout was caught weighing over nine pounds, and near Gisborne several have been caught approaching that size. In Lake Learmonth, in Beale's Swamp, and in other waters where fish have been placed by the Ballarat Society, trout turned out in 1872 have, through accident, been caught. These were found to weigh from two to three pounds when but thirteen months old, affording perhaps the best proof of the fitness of Victorian waters for them.

On the subject of trout in Beale's Swamp, a Ballarat observer writes :—

"We were seated on the embankment of this huge reservoir, watching a shoal of minnows in the clear water at our feet. The sun had dipped behind a dense cloud, and the faintest breeze gently stirred the dull, heavy atmosphere of the sultry evening, when a sudden and unaccountable movement of the minnows attracted our attention. The shoal were off like a shot! Two flashes of lightning, some three feet below the surface, with streaks of silver and gold! A cheer arose. All well knew what it meant—'big speckled fellows in Beale's!' We sat on the embankment until the sun disappeared, when we were again and again rewarded by sights of the fish. First one rather shy fellow came up, took a gnat and a look round, then, as if half-frightened at his own temerity, vanished to digest his dinner. Then a second, a lazy one, popped up, tried the flies, and as if saying to himself, ' Who's afraid !' indolently rolled himself over and over on the surface, showing his spotty splendour with great effect. Half-a-dozen more came up, and then ensued a regular fish corroboree—the trout rolling and tumbling about most playfully, and appearing to vary their *menage* now with flies and now with well fed minnows. We left the water at dusk, well satisfied with the glorious success of our acclimatisation in Beale's Swamp."

The fish in the ponds have thriven well, and are now five to six inches long, and must be gradually turned out to prevent overcrowding.

The ponds, which are designed upon the system adopted at Stormonfield, with such improvements as have been suggested by experience in Tasmania, were made from plans prepared by the writer, and carried out under the superintendence of Mr. Blackburn, the Shire Engineer of Gisborne. After nearly twelve months trial, no fault has been found or improvement suggested. The expense of construction was met by a special vote by the Victorian Parliament. The success which has so far attended the experiment is, however, mostly due to Mr. Robertson, who not only granted the site, but has, at his own cost, undertaken the care and management of the ponds, under the control and superintendence of the Society.

The ponds being situated near one of the main lines of railway, fish and ova may be easily and rapidly distributed to all parts of the colony.

The second or lower pond at Wooling has been devoted to, and is at present occupied by, some 200 salmon trout, hatched from ova presented by the Tasmanian Salmon Commissioners to the Society, and are the first salmon trout which have been introduced into the colony. They differ from the salmon in that although they visit the sea when available, they will live and breed without doing so; thus a yearly supply of young fish may be obtained. For sport and the table the salmon trout are by many deemed equal to the true salmon. Like the salmon, the young change from the par state to the smolt, and with the exception of those retained for breeding purposes, will be allowed to leave the pond when they arrive at that stage. They will gain access to the sea by the Deep Creek and Saltwater River; and if, as is believed, they succeed and return to fresh water, probably the result will be known sooner than has been the case in Tasmania, for not only are the waters through which they must pass narrower, but the fish can hardly pass up the fish ladders which they must ascend without being seen.

No time should now be lost in obtaining an Act of Parliament, similar to the Trout Act in Tasmania, embodying in it such clauses of the Salmon Act there as will be required for the protection of the salmon trout.

The next place must be given to the English perch : The history of their original introduction is not generally known, and may be interesting, as the result is almost incredible. During four successive years prior to 1861 attempts were made to introduce the perch to Tasmania from England, but it was not until December of that year that a fifth attempt succeeded, when—as in prior attempts—at Mr. Morton Allport's request and sole expense, the writer brought out under his personal charge and landed live fish, which were placed in ponds expressly built for them by Mr. Allport.

More fish were obtained by him the following year, from whence have sprung the immense supply now in Tasmania and Australia. To him, therefore—and to Mr. Joseph Allport, in whose gardens the ponds were built, and to whose unremitting care and attention is due the successful rearing of the parent fish—is the credit of stocking many thousands of acres of water, specially adapted for perch, and unfit perhaps for other valuable fish.

In the introduction of perch to Victoria, mention has again to be made of the Ballarat Society; and, in connection with it, of the Messrs. Seal, of Ballarat. Perch distributed by them now teem through the southern, the western, and the northern districts of the colony.

In Lake Wendouree, at Ballarat, no less than 9 tons have been caught during last season, yielding a large money value, some of the fish being of unusual size. The Ballarat Society has preserved a perch, caught in December last in that lake, which weighed 3½ lb. This fish was three years old. Another fish was caught there during the early part of this year (1874) which weighed 4 lb.

Visitors from England, who fished in the lake last season, say the sport there is superior to that in some of the best waters in England.

All the fish throughout the district spoken of are the produce of five small fishes caught in Tasmania, in 1868, by Mr. Morton Allport, and sent by him as a present to Messrs. Seal. Without them, Wendouree and other similar waters might perhaps have remained that which they were, "frogs' paradise," to the present day.

From Tasmania, and from Ballarat, the Society have received frequent supplies of perch, which have been distributed in various parts of the colony.

A pond was constructed at the Society's Gardens in the Royal Park for perch.

Prussian carp have been introduced by the Society. Tench also, and it is said Dace.

Roach have been introduced and caught in the Yarra, while those who prefer beauty to usefulness may indulge in a little fly fishing for goldfish in the same stream, where they are to be caught from 1 lb. weight upwards and downwards.

In concluding this report, it may be of use to those who have occasion to transport young fish, to describe an improvement which the Society adopts, on the plan suggested by the Tasmanian salmon commissioners in their reprint of Frank Buckland's "Hints on Fish Hatching and Fish Culture." It is to enclose all but the top of the tin in which the fish are carried, in an open net of wire, and over that with a tight-fitting canvas, such as buckets are made of; the space between the tin and the canvas being filled with water. The water in which the fish are is thus kept much cooler than it otherwise would be, especially in this climate.

Another improvement is to place a false bottom in the tin, concave in shape, so as not to present any crevice or corner into which fish may get; to pierce the false bottom with minute holes from the upper side, and to connect the space between the false and true bottom with a valve and piston at the side, to act as an air pump, to be worked with the fingers and thumb.

June 1874.

ADDITIONS

TO THE

LISTS OF THE PRINCIPAL TIMBER TREES AND OTHER SELECT PLANTS,

READILY ELIGIBLE FOR

VICTORIAN INDUSTRIAL CULTURE,

(Issued in 1871 and 1872 by the Acclimatisation Society).

OFFERED BY

BARON FERD. VON MUELLER,

C.M.G., M. & Ph.D., F.R.S.

In the first two volumes of the Proceedings of the Zoological and Acclimatisation Society of Victoria, notes on about 300 of the most important timber trees, and on about 700 species of other industrial plants were promulgated, with a view of affording some additional aid to colonists within our own territory, and perhaps also to inhabitants of other countries of a clime similar to ours, for choosing among the many thousands of predominantly utilitarian plants such species as can likely be grown to advantage in our geographic zone. On the occasions when these writings were issued, it was promised to offer from time to time supplements, comprising plants which in the first instance might have been overlooked, or which through more extended researches or new discoveries might have since become known or appreciated.

The first instalment of these additions is now submitted to the Society's supporters, and further supplemental notes may find their way perhaps also to publicity through the volumes of the Acclimatisation Society, so far as the scope

of its publications affords space for such purposes. Some
difficulty was again experienced on this occasion, not only in
the selection of the plants to be recommended, but also in the
limitation of the notes on any particular species. But not
every plant placed here is actually to be regarded as of proved
extensive industrial value ; or as of established remunerative
cultural yield ; on the contrary, in the majority of instances
they are only brought forward as recommendable for unbiassed
new and local tests by enlightened culturists. In reference
to the narrow boundaries, within which this and the two
former treatises have been held, it may be observed that, until
more voluminous writings of these kinds can appear through
special public provision, the very brief data, now additionally
brought together, may helpingly tend to the extension of
cultural experiments, to the augmentation of our foreign
intercourse for scientific industrial and mercantile purposes,
and to the increase of our rural wealth.

Melbourne, May 1874.

Aberia Caffra, Hooker.
    The Kai-Apple of Natal and Caffraria. This tall shrub serves
for hedges. The rather large fruits are edible, and can be
converted into preserves. Allied South African species are
A. Zeyheri and *A. tristis* (Sonder).

Acacia Arabica, Willdenow.
    Throughout Africa, also in South Asia. This small tree can be
utilized for thorny hedges, as also *A. Seyal* (Delile) and *A. tortilis*
(Forskael). They all furnish the best Gum Arabic for medicinal
and technical purposes. The Lac-Insect lives also on the foliage,
and thus in Sind the Lac is mainly yielded by this tree.

Acacia Concinna, Candolle.
    India. Praised by Dr. Cleghorn as a valuable hedge shrub. The
pod contains Saponin. So is likewise *A. latronum* (Willd.), a
hedge bush.

Acacia Cavenia, Hooker and Arnott.

The Espino of the present inhabitants of Chili, the Cavan of the former population. A small tree with exceedingly hard wood, resisting underground moisture. The plant is well adapted for hedges. The pods, called Quirinca, serve as cattle food (Dr. Philippi).

Acacia falcata, Willdenow.

East Australia. One of the best of trees for raising a woody vegetation on drift-sand, as particularly proved at the Cape of Good Hope. Other species serve the same purpose, for instance—*A. pycnantha, A. saligna, A. cyanophylla, A. salicina.*

Acacia fasciculifera, F. v. Mueller.

South Queensland. Desirable for culture on account of the excellence of its easily worked wood.

Acacia glaucescens, Willdenow.

Queensland and New South Wales. Extreme height, about 60 feet. A kind of Myall, with hard dark prettily grained but less scented wood.

Acacia harpophylla, F. v. Mueller.

Southern Queensland, where this tree, according to Mr. Thozet, furnishes a considerable share of the mercantile wattle-bark for tanning purposes. Wood, according to Mr. O'Shanesy, brown, hard, heavy and elastic, used by the natives for spears.

Acacia horrida, Willdenow.

The Doornboom or Karra-Doorn of South Africa. A formidable hedge bush with thorns three inches long, readily available for impenetrable hedge copses. It exudes also a good kind of gum. So *A. Giraffe* (Burchell).

Acacia lophantha, Willdenow.

South West Australia. One of the most rapidly growing trees for copses and first temporary shelter in exposed localities, but never attaining to the size of a real tree. It produces seeds abundantly, which germinate most easily. For the most desolate places, especially in desert tracts, it is of great importance to create quickly shade, shelter and copious vegetation. Cattle browse on the leaves. The bark contains only about 8 per cent. mimosa-tannin; but Mr. Rummel found in the dry root about 10 per cent. of saponin, valuable in silk and wool factories.

Acacia pendula, All. Cunningham.

New South Wales and Queensland. Generally in marshy tracts of the interior. One of the Myall trees.

Acacia pycnantha, Bentham.*

Victoria and South Australia. Though frequent in many parts of our colony, this tree, known as the Golden Wattle, deserves even here extensive cultivation, mainly for the sake of its bark, rich in tannin. It is of rapid growth, will succeed even in sandy tracts, and yields seeds copiously, which germinate with the greatest ease. It is never a large tree. By improved methods the fragrant oil of the flowers could doubtless be fixed, though its isolation might be difficult and unremunerative. Experiments in the writer's laboratory have shown that the perfectly dried bark contains about 25 per cent. of mimosa-tannin. The aqueous infusion of the bark can be reduced by boiling to a dry extract, which in medicinal and other respects is equal to the best Indian catechu, as derived from *Acacia catechu* and *A. sundra*. It yields approximately 30 per cent., about half of which or more is mimosa-tannic acid. This catechu is also of great use for preserving against decay articles subject to exposure in water, such as nets, fishing lines, &c. While according to Mr. Simmons the import of the bark of oaks and hemlock-spruce into England becomes every year less, and while the import of sumach and gambir does not increase, the annual demand has, since the last 20 years, become doubled. Probably no other tanning plants give so quick a return in cultivation than our *Acacia pycnantha* and particularly *A. ducurrens*. To the latter, the Black Wattle is already alluded in the list of timber trees; but the following additional notes may further show the importance of this neglected tree. The English price of the bark ranges generally from £8 to £11. It varies, so far as experiments under my direction have shown, in its contents of tannin from 18 to 33 per cent. In the mercantile bark the percentage is somewhat less, according to the state of its dryness—it retaining about 10 per cent. moisture. Any bare barren unutilized places might here be sown most remuneratively with the seeds of this Wattle Acacia, to secure a regular and continuous supply of the bark, which necessarily must fall off under the indiscriminate arrangements of obtaining the bark from the natural localities of growth. The return would be within very few years. 1¼ lb. of Black Wattle bark gives 1 lb. of leather, whereas 5 lb. of English Oak bark are requisite for the same results, but the tannin principle of both is not absolutely identical. The bark of the variety passing generally as the Silver Wattle (*Acacia dealbata, Link*), is generally of less value, often even fetching only half the price of that of the Black Wattle. The tannin of these Acaciæ yields a grey precipitate with the oxyd salts of iron, and a violet colour with sub-oxydes; it is completely thrown down from a strong aqueous solution by means of concentrated sulphuric acid. The bark improves by age and desiccation, and yields about 40 per cent. of catechu, rather more than half of which is tannic acid. Bichromate of potash added in a minute quantity to the boiling solution of mimosa-tannin produces a ruby-red liquid, fit for dye purposes, and this solution gives, with the salts of sub-oxyde of iron, black pigments; and with the salts of the full oxyde of iron, red-brown dyes.

Acacia saligna, Wendland.

South West Australia, where it is the principal tree chosen for tanner's bark. It is a widely spreading small tree, fit for avenues. The bark contains nearly 30 per cent. of mimosa-tannin.

Achillea moschata, Wulfen.

Alps of Europe. The Genipi or Iva of the alpine inhabitants. This perennial herb ought to be transferred to our snowy mountains. With the allied *A. nana (L.)* and *A. atrata (L.)*, it enters as a component into the aromatic medicinal Swiss tea. Many species of this genus, including the Yarrow, are wholesome to sheep. *A. fragrantissima (Reichenbach)*, is a shrubby species from the deserts of Egypt, valuable for its medicinal flowers.

Achras sapota, Linné.

The Sapodilla Plum of West India and Central Continental America. It is not improbable that this fine evergreen tree would produce its delicious fruit in East Gippsland within Victorian boundaries, as tall palms and many other plants of tropical type occur there. Moreover *Achras Australis*, a tree yielding also tolerably good fruit, occurs as far south as Kiama in New South Wales, where the clime is very similar to that of many forest regions of Victoria. Other sapotaceous trees, producing table fruit, such as the *Lucuma mammosa* (the Marmalade tree), *Lucuma Bonplandi*, *Chrysophyllum Cainito* (the Star apple), all from West India; and *Lucuma Caimito* of Peru might also be subjected to trial culture in our warmest forest valleys; so furthermore many of the trees of this order, from which guttapercha is obtained (species of *Isonandra, Sideroxylon, Ceratophorus, Cacosmanthus, Bassia, Mimusops* and *Imbricaria*), may prove hardy in our sheltered woodlands, as they seem to need rather an equable humid mild clime than the heat of the torrid zone.

Adenostemum nitidum, Persoon.

South Chili, where this stately tree passes by the appellations: *Quaule, Nuble* and *Arauco*. Wood durable and beautifully veined. Fruit edible.

Agaricus Cæsareus, Schaeffer.

In the spruce forests of Middle and South Europe. Trials might be made to naturalize this long-famed and highly delicious mushroom in our forests when spruce-fir plantations are made. It attains a width of nearly one foot, and is of a magnificent orange colour. Numerous other edible *Agarics* could doubtless be brought into these southern colonies by the mere dissemination of the spores at apt localities. As large or otherwise specially eligible may here be mentioned *A. extinctorius L.*, *A. melleus Vahl.*, *A. deliciosus L.*, *A. giganteus Sowerby*, *A. Cardarella, Fr.*, *A. Marzuolus Fr.*, *A. eryngii Cand.*, *A. splendens Pers.*, *A. odorus Bulliard*, *A. auricula Cand.*, *A. oreades Bolt.*, *A.*, *esculentus Wulf*, *A. mouceron Tratt.*, *A. socialis Cand.*, all from Europe, besides numerous other highly valuable species from other parts of the globe.

Agrostis rubra, Linné. (*A. borealis,* Hartmann.)

Northern Europe, Asia and America. A perennial grass called Red-top, and also Herd-grass in the United States of North America. Mr. Meehan places it for pastoral value among grasses cultivated there next after *Phleum pratense* and *Poa pratensis* (the latter there called Blue Grass), and before *Dactylis glomerata* (the Orchard Grass of the United States).

Aira cæspitosa, Linné.

Widely dispersed over the globe. A fair fodder-grass, best utilised for moist meadows.

Albizzia Lebbek, Bentham.

The Siris Acacia of South Asia. Available in the warmer parts of our colony as a shade-tree. It produces also a good deal of gum.

Allium roseum, Linné.

Countries on the Mediterranean Sea. This, with *Allium Neapolitanum* (Cyrillo), one of its companions, yields edible roots, according to Heldreich.

Aloexylon Agallochum, Loureiro.

Cochinchina, on the highest mountains; thus, this tree would probably prove hardy here. The precious Aloe-wood, so famed for its balsamic fragrance and medicinal properties, is derived from this tree.

Anthistiria avenacea, F. v. Mueller.

New South Wales and Queensland. A nutritious perennial pasture grass.

Amarantus Blitum, Linné.

South Europe, North Africa, South West Asia. This annual herb is a favourite plant among allied ones for spinage; but not only species of this genus, but also many other Amarantaceæ serve as culinary herbs.

Aponogeton distachyon, Thunberg.

South Africa. This curious water-plant, introduced already, might be naturalized in our ditches, swamps and lakes, for the sake of its edible tubers. The scented flowering portion affords spinage.

Aralia cordata, Thunberg.

China. The young shoots provide an excellent culinary vegetable.

Arbutus Menziesii, Pursh.

North-West America. An evergreen tree, attaining a height of 150 feet. It belongs to the coast-tract exclusively, Wood exceedingly hard. The tree requires a deep loamy soil (Bolander); it would here be valuable at least as a highly ornamental garden plant.

Aristolochia Indica, Linné.

Tropical Asia and Polynesia. A perennial climber; the leaves famed as an alexipharmic. Can only be grown in places free from frost.

Aristolochia recurvilabra, Hance.

The green Putchuck of China. A medicinal plant, largely obtained at Ningpo. The present value of its export is from £20,000 to £30,000 annually.

Artemisia Cina, Berg.

Kurdistan. This herb furnishes the genuine *Santonica* seeds (or rather flowers and fruits), as a vermifuge of long established use. Some other Asiatic species yield a similar drug.

Artemisia Mutellina, Villars.

Alps of Europe. This aromatic, somewhat woody plant deserves to be established in our snowy regions.

Artemisia Pontica, Linné.

Middle and South Europe, West Asia. More aromatic and less bitter than the ordinary wormwood. Many other species of this genus deserve attention of the culturist.

Arundo Ampelodesmos, Cyrillo.

South Europe, North Africa. Almost as large as *A. Gynerium*. The tough flower-stems and leaves readily available for tying.

Asparagus acutifolius, Linné.
In all the countries around the Mediterrean Sea, also in the Canary Islands. Although a shrubby Asparagus, yet the root-shoots, according to Dr. Heldreich, are collected in Greece, and are tender and of excellent taste, though somewhat thinner than those of the ordinary herbaceous species. The shrub grows on stony rises, and the shoots are obtained without cultivation. *A. aphyllus L.* and *A. horridus L.*, according to Dr. Reinhold, are utilized in the same manner, and all may probably yield an improved produce by regular and careful culture.

Asparagus laricinus, Burchell.
South Africa. Dr. Pappe observes of this shrubby species, that with some other kinds of that country, it produces shoots of excellent tenderness and aromatic taste.

Astragalus parnassi, Boissier.
(*A. Cylleneus*, Heldreich). Greece. This small shrub furnishes there almost exclusively the commercial Tragacanth. It ascends to elevations of 7000 feet, becomes therefore alpine.

Atalantia glauca, J. Hooker.
New South Wales and Queensland. This desert-lemon is mentioned here to draw attention to the likelihood of its improving in culture, and to its fitness of being grown in arid land.

Atriplex nummularium, Lindley.
From Queensland through the desert-tracts to Victoria and South Australia. One of the tallest and most fattening and wholesome of our pastoral salt-bushes, and although a native plant even here highly recommendable for artificial rearing, as the spontaneously growing plants, by close occupation of the sheep and cattle runs, have largely disappeared, and as this useful bush even here in many wide tracts does not exist.

Atriplex spongiosum, F. v. Mueller.
Through a great part of Central Australia, extending to the west-coast. Available like the preceding, and like *A. halimoides*, *A. holocarpum* and several other species for saltbush culture.

Avena elatior, Linné.
Europe, Middle Asia, North Africa. This tall grass should not be passed altogether on this occasion, although it becomes easily irrepressible on account of its wide creeping roots. It should here be chosen for dry and barren tracts of country, it having proved to resist our occasional droughts even better than Rye-grass. The bulk yielded by it is great, it submits well to

depasturing, and gives two or three crops of hay annually: it is however not so much relished by animals as many other grasses.

Averrhoa Carambola, Linné.
Insular India. Dr. Hooker having found this small tree on the Upper Indus as far as Lahore, it may reasonably be anticipated that success would attend its rearing in the warmest and moistest parts of our colonial territory. The fruit occurs in a sweet and acid variety; the former is raw available for the table, the other for preserves. That of *A. Bilimbi* (Linné) is of similar use.

Azima tetracantha, Lamarck.
From South India to South Africa. A hedge-bush, growing freely in every kind of soil.

Baccharis pilularis, Candolle.
California. This evergreen bush, like *B. consanguinea*, is grown for hedges, used also for garlands, wrappers of flower bouquets and many decorative purposes, as cut branches do not wither for a considerable time. It attains a height of 15 feet (Professor Bolander).

Backhousia citriodora, F. v. Mueller.
South Queensland. Though only a small tree it is well worth cultivating for the fragrance of its lemon-scented foliage.

Balsamodendron Ehrenbergi, Berg.
Deserts of Arabia. This tree yields the Myrrha resin, but perhaps some other species may produce the same substance. Professor Oliver unites this with the following species.

Balsamodendron Opobalsamum, Kunth. (*B. Gileadense*, Kunth,)
Arabia and Nubia. This species furnishes Mekka or Gilead Balsam. *B. Capense* (Sonder) is a closely allied species from extratropical South Africa. Many other Balsam shrubs deserve introduction.

Balsamodendron Mukul, Hooker.
Scindo and Beludschistan. Yields the Bdellium resin.

Basella lucida, Linné.
India. Perennial. This spinage-plant has somewhat the odour of *Ocimum Basilicum*; other species serve also culinary purposes.

Basella rubra, Linné.
From South Asia to Japan. This annual or biennial herb serves as a spinage of pleasant coloration.

Benincasa cerifera, Savi.
> India. This annual plant produces a large edible gourd, which in an unripe state forms part of the composition of many kinds of currie.

Berberis Asiatica, Roxburgh.
> Himalaya. One of the best among numerous species with edible berries. Among these may specially be mentioned *B. lycium* (Royle) and *B. aristata* (Candolle), which also yield valuable yellow dye wood (Dr. Rosenthal).

Berberis Darwinii, Hooker.
> Chiloe and South Chili. Considered one of the most handsome of all shrubs for garden hedges. Several other evergreen Berbery shrubs serve the same purpose.

Betula lutea, Michaux.
> The yellow or grey Birch of North-East America. Adapted for moist forest land. In size and most other respects similar to *B. lenta.*

Bongardia Rauwolfi, C. A. Meyer.
> From Greece through Turkey to the Caucasus. A perennial herb, the leaves of which are utilized like culinary sorrel.

Boswellia papyrifera, A. Richard.
> Morocco, Nubia, and Abyssinia, forming entire forests about Bertat on the Atlas. This tree exudes a kind of olibanum resin and represents apparently one of the hardest species of this and allied genera.

Brassica juncea, J. Hook and Thoms. (*B. Willdenowii, Boiss Sinapis juncea,* Linné.)
> From Middle Africa to China. According to Colonel Drury, cultivated all over India for sarepta mustard seeds; also a good salad plant.

Brassica chinensis, Linné.
> China and Japan. Serves like the following for cabbage, and may in cultivation produce new varieties. *B. cretica* (Lam.), a woody mediterranean species.

Butea frondosa, Roxburgh.
> The Dhak or Pulas of India. This magnificent tree extends to the Himalayan mountains, and therefore might here be a proper one for acclimatisation. It is very rich in a peculiar kind of kino. The Lac-insect is also nourished by this tree, and might be transferred to us with it.

Buchloa dactyloides, Torrey.*

The true Buffalo-grass of Kansas. Diœcious, creeping, only rising to half a foot or less. It is extremely fattening, but apt to be suppressed by coarser grasses on places where these are not trampled out or kept down by the pasture animals.

Buddleya Madagascariensis, Lamarck.

Madagascar. Of the numerous species of Buddleya, the most eligible for shelter copses on account of its great size and always tidy appearance, as well as vigour and celerity of growth. It is ever flowering.

Buxus sempervirens, Linné.

The Turkey Box-tree. South Europe, North Africa, South-West Asia. This slow growing tree should timely be planted, to provide the indispensable box-wood for wood engravers and musical instrument makers, as yet no good substitute for it having been discovered. The box-tree needs calcareous soil for its best development. Among allied species *B. Balearica* attains a height of 80 feet. Other congeners are *B. subcolumellaris, B. Cubana, B. Purdieana, B. citrifolia, B. acuminata, B. lævigata, B. Vahlii, B. gonoclada, B. retusa, B. glomerata, B. Wrightii,* all from West India; further, *B. Madagascarica, B. longifolia* from Turkey, *B. Wallichiana* from the Himalayas and *B. microphylla* from Japan, but neither of any of these, nor of the various species of the allied Indian genus *Sarcococca,* nor of several species of the Andine genus *Styloceras,* does it appear to be known what relation their wood may hold to that of the true box-tree, and whether they are more rapid in growth.

Cæsalpinia coriaria, Willdenow.

Wet sea shores of Central America. Might be naturalised in our salt marshes. Colonel Drury states, that each full grown tree produces annually about 100 lbs. of pods, the husk of which, commercially known as Divi-Divi, is regarded as the most powerful and quickly acting tanning material in India. The mercantile price of the pods is from £8 to £13 per ton.

Cæsalpinia Sappan, Linné.

South Asia. The wood furnishes red dye. This shrub can also be utilized for hedges. It would likely prove hardy here in places free of frost.

Cæsalpinia sepiaria, Roxburgh.

South Asia, east to Japan. Can be utilized in the warmer tracts of our colony as a hedge bush. It can advantageously be mixed for hedge growth with *Pterolobium laceruns* (R. Br.), according to Dr. Cleghorn.

Cæsalpinia tinctoria, Humboldt.
Chili. The bark yields a red dye.

Calamagrostis longifolia, Hooker.
North America. Excellent for fixing drift sand.

Calamintha Nepeta, Hoffmansegg.
Is of the strongest odour among several species, but not of so pleasant a scent as *C. incana* (Boiss) and *C. grandiflora* (Moench).

Calamintha officinalis, Moench.
Middle and South Europe and middle Asia, North Africa. A perennial herb, used like *melissa* as a condiment.

Calyptranthes aromatica, St. Hilaire.
South Brazil. This spice shrub would likely prove hardy here, the flower-buds can be used almost like cloves, the berries like allspice. Several other aromatic species are eligible for test culture.

Capparis sepiaria, Linné.
From India to the Philippine Islands, ascending to cool elevations and living in arid soil. A prickly bush, excellent for hedges. Dr. Cleghorn mentions also as hedge plants *C. horrida* (L. fil.), *C. aphylla* (Roth), *C. Roxburghii* (Cand.), some of which yield also capers.

Caragana arborescens, Lamarck.
The Pea-tree of Siberia. The seeds are of culinary value, but particularly used for feeding fowl. The leaves yield a blue dye (Dr. Rosenthal).

Carex arenaria, Linné.
Europe and North Asia. One of the most powerful of sedges for subduing rolling sand, not attracting pasture animals by its foliage.

Carissa Arduina, Lamarck.
South Africa. A shrub with formidable thorns, well adapted for boundary lines of gardens, where rapidity of growth is not an object. Quite hardy at Melbourne. *C. ferox* (E. Meyer) and *C. grandiflora* (A de Cand.), are allied plants of equal value. The East Australian, *C. Brownii* (F. von Mueller) can be similarly utilized. The flowers of all are very fragrant. *C. Carandas* (Linné), extends from India to China; its berries are edible.

Carum nigrum, Royle.
Himalaya. With *C. gracile* this yields caraway like fruits.

Carum Bulbocastanum, Koch.
Middle and South Europe, North Africa, Middle Asia, on limestone soil. The tuberous roots serve as a culinary vegetable, the fruits as a condiment.

Carum Capense, Sonder.
South Africa, where the edible, somewhat aromatic root is called Fenkelwortel.

Carum segetum, Bentham, (*Anethum segetum*, Linné).
Around the Mediterranean Sea, extending to Middle Europe. An aromatic annual herb, available for culinary purposes.

Cassia fistula, Linné.
South Asia. The long pods of this ornamental tree contain an aperient pulp of pleasant taste. Traced by Dr. Hooker to the dry slopes of the central Himalayas.

Casuarina Decaisneana, F. v. Mueller.
Central Australia, where it is the only species of the genus. This tree is one of the largest among its congeners, and particularly valuable for arid regions.

Casuarina torulosa, Aiton.
New South Wales and Queensland. The wood of this handsome tree is in demand for durable shingles and furniture work; it is also one of the best for oven fuel.

Castaneopsis chrysophylla, A. de Candolle.
The Oak-Chesnut of California and Oregon. A tree attaining a large size of beautiful outlines. The leaves are golden yellow underneath. Wood durable.

Catalpa bignonioides, Walter.
On the Gulf of Mexico. A tree in warm humid climatic zones of remarkable celerity of growth. Mr. Meehan regards the wood to be as durable as that of the best chesnut trees, and observed a stem in twenty years to attain a diameter of three feet, even in the clime of New York.

Ceanothus rigidus, Nuttall.
California. One of the best of hedge shrubs, available for dry situations. Evergreen; up to 12 feet high; the branches become densely intricate. In the coast-tracts it is replaced by *C. thyrsiflorus, Esch.*, which can also be used for hedges and copses, and will live in mere coast-sand. *C. prostratus, Benth.*, likes to form natural mats on slopes formed by roads and slides, which it gradually covers, and with its pretty blue flowers soon decorates (Professor Bolander).

Cercocarpus ledifolius, Nuttall.
California. Rises in favourable spots to a tree 40 feet high, with a stem diameter of 2½ feet. The wood is the hardest known in California. *C. parvifolius* is of lesser dimensions.

Chærophyllum bulbosum, Linné.
Europe and Middle Asia. The root forms a kitchen vegetable. Several other species yield edible roots.

Chenopodium blitum, F. von Mueller. (*Blitum virgatum*, Linné).
From South Europe to India. An annual herb, extensively in use there as a cultivated spinage-plant. The fruits furnish a red dye. The genus *Blitum* was reduced to *chenopodium* by the writer in Caruel's *Giornale Botanico* some years ago. *C. capitatum* (*Blitum capitatum*, L.) may not be really a distinct species. *C. Quinoa*, Willd., from Chili, deserves hardly recommendation for culture, though a nutritious spinage, it being apt to stray as a weed into cultivated fields. Some of these sorts of plants are useful to anglers, as attracting fish, when thrown into rivers or lakes.

Chrogalum pomeridianum, Kunth.
California, frequent on the mountains. This lily-like plant attains a height of 8 feet. The heavy bulb is covered with many coatings, consisting of fibres, which are used for cushions, mattresses, etc.; large contracts are entered into for the supply of this material on a very extensive scale (Professor Bolander). The inner part of the bulb serves as a substitute for soap, and it might be tried whether it can be utilized for technological purposes like the root of Saponaria.

Chloroxylon Swietenia, Candolle.
The Satin wood. Mountains of India. Like the allied *Flindersias*, possibly this tree would prove hardy here in naturally sheltered places, the cognate *Cedrela Taona* advancing in East Australia southward to the 35th degree. A resin, valuable for varnishes, exudes from the stem and branches.

Chrysanthemum roseum, Adam.
South-West Asia. This perennial herb, with *C. carneum*, yields the Persian insect powder.

Cinna arundinacea, Linné.
North America. There recorded as a good fodder grass; perennial, somewhat sweet-scented. *Blyttia suaveolens* (Fries) is, according to Dr. Asa Gray, a variety with pendant flowers.

Cistus creticus, Linné.
   Countries at the Mediterranean Sea. This shrub, with *C. cyprius* (Lam.), furnishes the best Ladanum resin. Other species yield a less fragrant product.

Combretum butyraceum, Caruel.
   The Butter tree of Caffraria and other parts of South-East Africa. The Caffirs call the fatty substance obtained from this tree *Chiquito*. It is largely used by them as an admixture to their food, and exported also. It contains about one quarter Olein and three quarters Margarin. This butterlike fat is extracted from the fruit, and is of an aromatic flavour. The tree should be hardy in the warmer and milder parts of Victoria.

Cordyline Ti, Schott.
   China. The roots in a roasted state are edible. The leaves, like those of other species, can be utilized for textile fibre.

Crambe cordifolia, Steven.
   From Persia and the Caucasus to Thibet and the Himalayas up to 14,000 feet. The root and foliage of this Kale afford an esculent. *C. Kotschyana* (Boiss.) is an allied plant.

Cratægus Azarolus, Linné.
   Welsh Medlar. South Europe and South-West Asia. The pleasantly acidulous fruits are much used for preserves.

Crocus serotinus, Salisbury. (*C. odorus,* Bivona).
   South Europe. Also this species produces Saffron rich in pigment. The bulbs of several are edible.

Cudrania Javensis, Trecul.
   New South Wales and Queensland, South and East Asia to Japan, East Africa. This climbing thorny shrub can be utilized for hedges. Fruit edible, of pleasant taste; the root furnishes a yellow dye.

Cymopterus glomeratus, Candolle.
   Western States of North America. Root edible (Dr. Rosenthal).

Cynodon Dactylon, Persoon.*
   Widely dispersed over the warmer parts of the globe, thus as indigenous reaching the northern parts of our colony. An important grass for covering bare barren land, or binding drift sand, or keeping together the soil of abrupt declivities, or consolidating earth-banks against floods. It is not without value as a pasture-grass, resists extreme drought, and may become of great importance to many desert tracts. The dispersion is best

effected by the creeping rooting stems, cut into short pieces; each of these takes root readily. In arable land this grass, when once established, cannot easily be subdued. The stems and roots are used in Italy for preparing there the *Mellago graminis*. Roxburgh already declared this grass to be by far the most common and useful of India, that it flowers all the year, and that it forms three-fourths of the food of the cows and horses there.

Danthonia Cunninghami, J. Hooker.
New Zealand. A splendid alpine fodder grass with large panicles.

Danthonia nervosa, J. Hooker.
Extra-tropic Australia. One of the best of nutritious swamp grasses.

Danthonia pectinata, Lindley.
New South Wales, Queensland and North Australia, in the arid interior regions. A perennial desert-grass, resisting drought; sought with avidity by sheep, and very fattening to them.

Danthonia triticoides, Lindley.
Of nearly the same natural distribution as the preceding, and equalling that species in value. Both so important as to deserve rearing even in their native countries.

Debregeasia edulis, Weddell.
The *Janatsi-itsigo* or *Toon-itsigo* of Japan. Berries of this bush edible, fibre valuable for textile fabrics. A few Indian species, with fibre resembling that of *Boehmeria*, ascend to the Himalayas for several thousand feet, and may therefore be hardy here, namely, *D. velutina*, *D. Wallichiana*, *D. hypoleuca*; the latter extends to Abyssinia, where it has been noticed at elevations of 8000 feet. On mountains in Java occurs *D. dichotoma*.

Desmodium triflorum, Candolle.
In tropical regions of Asia, Africa and America. A densely matted perennial herb, alluded to on this occasion as recommendable for places too hot for ordinary clover, and as representing a large genus of plants, many of which may prove of pastoral value. Dr. Roxburgh already stated that it helps to form the most beautiful turf in India, and that cattle are very fond of this herb. Colonel Drury informs us, that it is springing up in all soils and situations, supplying there the place of *Trifolium* and *Medicago*.

Dioscorea quinqueloba, Thunberg.

Japan, and there one of several yam plants with edible tubers. Among numerous congeners are mentioned as providing likewise root vegetables: *D. piperifolia* (Humboldt) from *Quito*, *D. esurientum* (Fenzl) from *Guatemala*, *D. tuberosa* and *D. conferta* (Vellozo) from South Brazil, *D. Cayennensis* (Lamarck) from tropical South America, *D. triphylla* (Linné) from tropical Asia, *D. deltoidea* (Wallich) from Nepal. Of these and many other species the relative quality of the roots, and the degree of facility but their field cultivation require to be more ascertained.

Diospyros Ebenum, Retzius.*

Ceylon, where it furnishes the best kind of Ebony wood. It is not uncommon up to 5000 feet in that island, according to Dr. Thwaites, hence I would recommend this large and valuable tree for test plantations in East Gippsland, and in other lowland forest regions of our colony, where also *D. quæsita* and *D. oppositifolia* (Thwaites), the best Calamander trees and *D. Melanoxylon*, should be tried. Many other species of *Diospyros* could probably be introduced from the mountains of various tropical regions, either for the sake of their ebony-like wood or their fruit.

Diospyros Lotus, Linné.

From Northern China to the Caucasus. The ordinary Date plum. The sweet fruits of this tree, resembling black cherries, are edible, and also used for the preparation of syrup. The wood, like that of *D. chloroxylon*, is known in some places as green Ebony; it must however not be confounded with other, such as are furnished by some species of *Excæcaria*, *Nectandra* and *Jacaranda*.

Dolichos uniflorus, Lamarck.

Tropical and sub-tropical Africa and Asia. An annual herb, well adapted for stable pulse.

Drimys Winteri, R. and G. Forster.

Extra tropical South America. The *Canelo* of Chili, sacred under the name of *Boighe* to the original inhabitants. Attains in river valleys a height of 60 feet. The wood never attacked by insects (Dr. Philippi); thus the Australian species may be equally valuable.

Elæagnus parvifolius, Royle.

From China to the Himalayas. This bush has been introduced as a hedge plant into North America, and, according to Mr. Meehan, promises great permanent success, as it achieved already a high popularity in this respect. Several other species might well be experimented on in the same manner.

Elegia nuda, Kunth.

South Africa. A rush able with its long root to bind moving sand; it also affords good material for thatching (Dr. Pappe). Many of the tall *Restiaceæ* of South Africa would prove valuable for scenic effect in the gardens and conservatories, and among these may specially be mentioned *Cannamois cephalotes* (Beauv.)

Embothrium coccineum, R. and G. Forster.

From Chili to Magellan's Straits. The *Notra* or *Ciruelillo* of Chili. A tree of exquisite beauty, but seldom extending to beyond 30 feet in height. The wood is utilized for furniture. *E. lanceolatum* is merely a variety (Dr. Philippi). The equally gorgeous *E. emarginatum* of the Peruvian Andes, and *E. Wickhami* from Mount Bellenden Ker of North Queensland deserve, with the East Australian allied *Stenocarpus sinuatus*, a place in any sheltered gardens or parks of the warm temperate zone.

Encephalartos Denisonii, F. v. Mueller.

New South Wales and Queensland. This noble pine palm is hardy here, and to be regarded as a most desirable acquisition to our garden sceneries, along with *E. spiralis*, *E. Preissii* and the South African species. All admit of translocation even when of large size and when many years old. The stems, with an unusual tenacity of life, remain sometimes dormant after removal for several years.

Eucalyptus acmenoides, Schauer.

New South Wales and East Queensland. The wood used in the same way as that of *E. obliqua* (the stringy bark tree), but superior to it. It is heavy, strong, durable, of a light colour, and has been found good for palings, flooring-boards, battens, rails, and many other purposes of house carpentry (Rev. Dr. Woolls).

Eucalyptus botryoides, Smith.

From East Gipps Land to South Queensland. One of the most stately among an extensive number of species, remarkable for its dark green shady foliage. It delights on river banks. Stems attain a length of 80 feet without a branch, and a diameter of 8 feet. The timber usually sound to the centre, adapted for water work, waggons, knees of boats, etc. Posts of it very lasting, as no decay was observed in fourteen years.

Eucalyptus brachypoda, Turczaninow.

Widely dispersed over the most arid extra-tropical as well as tropical inland regions of Australia. One of the best trees for desert tracts; in favourable places 150 feet high. Wood brown,

sometimes very dark, hard, heavy and elastic, prettily marked;
thus used for cabinet work, but more particularly for piles,
bridges and railway sleepers (Rev. Dr. Woolls).

Eucalyptus calophylla, R. Brown.

South West Australia. More umbrageous than most Eucalypts
and of comparatively rapid growth. The wood is free of resin
when grown on alluvial land, but not so when produced on
stony ranges. It is preferred to that of *E. marginata* and *E. cornuta*
for rafters, spokes and fence rails; it is strong and light, but
not long lasting underground. The bark is valuable for tanning,
as an admixture to *Acacia* bark.

Eucalyptus cornuta, La Billardiere.

South West Australia. A large tree of rapid growth, preferring
a somewhat humid soil. The wood is used for various artisans'
work, and there preferred for the strongest shafts and frames of
carts and other work requiring hardness, toughness and
elasticity.

Eucalyptus crebra, F. v. Mueller.

The narrow-leaved iron-bark tree of New South Wales and
Queensland. Wood reddish, hard, heavy, elastic and durable,
much used in the construction of bridges, also for waggons, piles,
fencing, etc. *E. melanophloia* (F. v. M.), the silver leaved iron-
bark tree, and *E. leptophleba*, *E. trachyphloia* and *E. drepanphylla*
are closely allied species of similar value. They all exude
astringent gum-resin in considerable quantity, resembling kino
in appearance and property.

Eucalyptus Doratoxylon, F. v. Mueller.

The spear-wood of South-west Australia, where it occurs in
sterile districts. The stem is slender and remarkably straight,
and the wood of such firmness and elasticity, that the nomadic
natives wander long distances to obtain it as material for their
spears.

Eucalyptus eugenioides, Sieber.

New South Wales. Regarded by the Rev. Dr. Woolls as a fully
distinct species. Its splendid wood, there often called blue-gum
tree wood, available for many purposes, and largely utilized for
ship building.

Eucalyptus Gunnii, J. Hooker.

Victoria, Tasmania and New South Wales, at alpine and subalpine elevations. The other more hardy Eucalypts comprise
E. coriacea, *E. alpina*, *E. urnigera*, *E. coccifera* and *E. vernicosa*,
which all reach heights covered with snow for several months in
the year.

Eucalyptus goniocalyx, F. v. Mueller.
From Cape Otway to the southern parts of New South Wales. A large tree which should be included among those for new plantations. Its wood resembles in many respects that of *E. globulus*. For house building, fence rails and similar purposes it is extensively employed in those forest districts where it is abundant, and has proved itself a valuable timber.

Eucalyptus hemiphloia, F. v. Mueller.
New South Wales and South Queensland. To be regarded as a timber tree of great excellence, on the authority of the Rev. Dr. Woolls. It is famous for the hardness and toughness of its timber, which is used for shafts, spokes, plough beams and similar utensils.

Eucalyptus Leucoxylon, F. v. Mueller.
The ordinary iron-bark tree of Victoria and some parts of South Australia and New South Wales. As the supply of its very durable timber is falling short, and as it is for some purposes superior to that of almost any other *Eucalypt*, the regular culture of this tree over wide areas should be fostered, especially as it can be raised on stony ridges not readily available for ordinary husbandry. The wood is sometimes pale, or in other localities rather dark. The tree is generally restricted to the lower Silurian sandstone, and slate formation with ironstone and quartz. It is rich in Kino. *E. siderozylon* is a synonym.

Eucalyptus maculata, Hooker.
The spotted gum tree of New South Wales and South Queensland. A lofty tree, the wood of which is employed in ship-building, wheelwrights' and coopers' work. The heartwood as strong as that of British Oak (Rev. Dr. Woolls).

Eucalyptus obliqua, L'Heritier.*
The ordinary Stringybark tree, attaining gigantic dimensions. The most extensively distributed and most gregarious of all Eucalypts, from Spencer's Gulf to the southern parts of New South Wales, and in several varieties designated by splitters and other wood-workers by different names; most extensively used for cheap fencing rails, palings, shingles and any other rough wood work, not to be sunk underground nor requiring great strength or elasticity. The bulk of wood obtained from this tree in very poor soil is perhaps larger than that of any other kind, and thus this species can be included even here, where it is naturally common and easily redisseminated, among the trees for new forest plantations in barren woodless tracts of our own country, to yield readily and early a supply of cheap and easily fissile wood.

Eucalyptus paniculata, Smith.

The White Iron-bark tree of New South Wales. All the trees of this series are deserving of cultivation, as their wood, though always excellent, is far from alike, and that of each species preferred for special purposes of the artisans.

Eucalyptus Phœnicea, F. v. Mueller.*

Carpentaria and Arnheim's Land. Of the quality of the timber hardly anything is known, but the brilliancy of its scarlet flowers recommends this species to a place in any forest or garden plantation. For the same reason also, *E. miniata,* from North Australia, and *E. ficifolia,* from South-West Australia, should be brought extensively under cultivation.

Eucalyptus pilularis, Smith.

The Black-butt tree of South Queensland, New South Wales and Gipps Land. One of the best timber yielding trees about Sydney, of rather rapid growth (Rev. Dr. Woolls). It is much used for flooring boards.

Eucalyptus platyphylla, F. v. Mueller.

Queensland. Regarded by the Rev. Julian Tenison Woods as one of the best of shade trees, and seen to produce leaves sometimes 1¼ foot long and 1 foot wide. This tree is available for open exposed localities, where trees from deep forest valleys would not thrive.

Eucalyptus robusta, Smith.

New South Wales. The timber in use for ship building, wheelwrights' work and many implements, such as mallets, etc.

Eucalyptus resinifera, Smith.

The Red Mahogany Eucalypt of South Queensland and New South Wales. A superior timber tree, according to the Rev. Dr. Woolls, the wood being much prized for its strength and durability.

Eucalyptus siderophloia, Bentham.*

The large leaved or red Iron-bark tree of New South Wales and South Queensland. According to the Rev. Dr. Woolls this furnishes one of the strongest and most durable timbers of New South Wales; with great advantage used for railway sleepers and for many building purposes. It is harder even than the wood of *E. Sideroxylon,* but thus also worked with more difficulty.

Eucalyptus tereticornis, Smith.*

From East Queensland to Gipps Land. Closely allied to *E. rostrata* and seemingly not inferior to it in value.

Eucalyptus tesselaris, F. v. Mueller.
North Australia and Queensland. Furnishes a brown, rather elastic wood, not very hard, available for many kinds of artisans' work, and particularly sought for staves and flooring. The tree exudes much astringent gum resin (P. O'Shanesy). Many other Eucalypts could have been mentioned as desirable for wood culture, but it would have extended this enumeration beyond the limits assigned to it. Moreover, the quality of many kinds is not yet sufficiently ascertained, or not yet fully appreciated even by the artisans and woodmen.

Eucryphia cordifolia, Cavanilles.
The Muermo or Ulmo of Chili. This magnificent evergreen tree attains a height of over 100 feet, producing a stem of sometimes 6 feet diameter. The flowers are much sought by bees. For oars and rudders the wood is preferred in Chili to any other. (Dr. Philippi.) We possess congeneric trees in Tasmania (*E. Billardieri*) and in New South Wales (*E. Moorei*).

Eugenia cordifolia, Wight.
Ceylon, up to 3,000 feet high. Fruit of one inch diameter.

Eugenia Hallii, Berg.
Quito. Fruit of large size.

Eugenia maboides, Wight.
Ceylon, up to 7,000 feet elevation. Fruit of the size of a small cherry (Dr. Thwaites).

Eugenia Malaccensis, Linné.
The large rose apple, India. Although strictly a tropical tree, it has been admitted into this list as likely adapted for our warmer forest regions. The leaves are often a foot long. The large fruits of rosy odour are wholesome and of agreeable taste. *E. Jambos, L.*, also from India, produces likewise excellent fruit.

Eugenia Nhanica, Cambessedes.
South Brazil. The berries, which are of plum size, are there a table fruit.

Eugenia pyriformis, Cambessedes.
Uvalho do Campo of South Brazil. Fruit of pear size.

Eugenia revoluta, Wight.
Ceylon, up to heights of 6,000 feet, berry one inch in diameter.

Eugenia rotundifolia, Wight.
Ceylon, up to 8,000 feet, rejoicing therefore in a cool or even cold climate.

Eugenia supra-axillaris, Spring.
>The Tata of South Brazil. Fruit large.

Eugenia Zeyheri, Harvey.
>South Africa. A tree attaining 20 feet height. The berries are of cherry size and edible. The relative value of the fruits of many Asiatic, African and American species of *Eugenia* remains to be ascertained; many of them furnish doubtless good timber, and all more or less essential oil; some probably also superior fruit. All such, even tropical trees, should be tested in East Gipps Land and other warm tracts of our colony, inasmuch as many of them endure a cooler clime than is generally supposed. Hence *Anona muricata* (*L.*), the Soursop Bush of West India, should also be subjected to test culture for the yield of its sweet fragrant melon-like fruit, and not less so *Anona squamosa* (*L.*), the Sweetsop shrub or tree of Central America, for the sake of its very pleasant fruit.

Euryale ferox, Salisbury.
>From tropical Asia to Japan. Though less magificent than the grand Victoria Regia, this closely allied waterlily is much more hardy, and would live unprotected in ponds and lakes of our colony. Though not strictly an industrial plant, it is not without utility, and undergoes some sort of cultivation in China for yielding its edible root and seeds.

Euryangium Sumbul, Kaufmann.
>Central Asia. Yields the true Sumbul root.

Fagus Dombeyi, Mirbel.
>The evergreen beech of Chili, called there the Coigue or Coihue. Of grand dimensions. Canoes out of its stem can be obtained of a size to carry ten tons freight. The wood is still harder than that of the following species, with the qualities of which it otherwise agrees (Dr. Philippi). This species extends to the Chonos group and perhaps still further south, and thus might be of value even for middle European forest culture.

Fagus obliqua, Mirbel.
>The Roble of Chili, called Coyam by the original inhabitants. A tall tree with a straight stem, attaining 3 to 4 feet diameter. Wood heavy and durable, well adapted for posts, beams, girders, rafters, joists, etc., but not for flooring. One of the few Chilian trees with deciduous foliage (Dr. Philippi). Its value as compared to that of the European beech should in our forest plantations be tested.

Fagus procera, Poeppig.
Another deciduous beech of Chili, where it passes by the names *Reulé* or *Rauli*. Of still more colossal size than the Roble. Wood fissile, but well adapted for staves; it is finer in grain than that of *F. obliqua*, and much used for furniture (Dr. Philippi).

Ferula longifolia, Fischer.
South Russia. The aromatic long roots furnish a pleasant vegetable (Dr. Rosenthal).

Festuca coiron, Steudel.
Chili. A valuable perennial fodder grass, according to the testimony of Dr. Philippi.

Festuca distichophylla, J. Hooker.
Victoria, South Australia, Tasmania, New South Wales. This dwarf creeping grass is of great value for binding soil, forming rough lawns, edging garden plots on arid places, and covering coast sand.

Festuca dives, F. v. Mueller.*
Victoria, from West Gipps Land to Dandenong and the sources of the rivers Yarra and Goulburn. One of the most magnificent of all sylvan grasses, not rarely 12 feet and exceptionally to 17 feet high. Root perennial. This grass deserves to be brought to any forest tracts, as it prospers in shade; along rivulets in deep soil it assumes its grandest forms. The large panicle affords nutritious forage.

Festuca flava, F. v. Mueller. (*Poa flava, Gronov, Tricuspis seslerioides, Torr., Uralepis cuprea,* Kunth).
The tall redtop-grass of the Eastern States of North America. A perennial sand-grass, with wide panicles.

Festuca gigantea. Villars.
Europe and Middle Asia. A perennial good forest-grass.

Festuca heterophylla, Lamarck.
Mountains of Europe. This perennial grass attains a height of five feet; it produces a proportionately great bulk of fodder, and serves as an admixture to grasses of hay or pasture lands, particularly the former (Lawson). It is best fitted for our alpine and highest forest-tracts, which in course of time and perhaps early so, will be sought for close pastoral occupation, when territorial areas will become less easily acquired.

Festuca spadicea, Linné.
Alps of Europe. This grass would thrive on the heights of our snowy mountains. Perennial.

Festuca purpurea, F. v. Mueller. (*Uralepis purpurea*, Nutt., *Tricuspis purpurea*, A. Gray).

South East coast of North America. A tufty sand grass, but annual.

Festuca silvatica, Villars.

Middle and South Europe. A notable forest-grass. *F. drymeia* (Mert. and Koch), a grass with long creeping roots, is closely allied. Both deserve here test culture.

Ficus columnaris, Moore and Mueller.

The Banyan tree of Lord Howe's Island, therefore extratropical. One of the most magnificent productions in the whole empire of plants. Mr. Fitzgerald, a visitor to the island, remarks that the pendulous air-roots, when they touch the ground, gradually swell into columns of the same dimensions as the older ones, which already become converted into stems, so that it is not apparent which was the parent trunk; there may be a hundred of stems to the tree on which the huge dome of dark evergreen foliage rests, but these stems are all alike, and thus it is impossible to say whence the tree comes or whither it goes. The allied fig trees of continental East Australia have great buttresses, but only now and then a pendulous root, approaching in similarity the stems of *Ficus columnaris*. The Lord Howe's Island fig-tree is more like *F. macrophylla* than *F. rubiginosa;* but *F. columnaris* is more rufous than either. In humid, warm sheltered tracts of Victoria, this grand vegetable living structure may be raised as an enormous bower for shade and for scenic ornament. The nature of the sap, whether available for caoutchouc or other industrial material, requires yet to be tested.

Ficus Cunninghami, Miquel.

Queensland, in the Eastern dense forest regions. Mr. O'Shanesy designates this as a tree of sometimes monstrous growth, the large spreading branches sending down roots which take firm hold of the ground. One tree measured was 38 feet in circumference at two feet from the ground, the roots forming wall-like abutments, some of which extended 20 feet from the tree. Several persons could conceal themselves in the large crevices of the trunk, while the main branches stretched across a space of about 100 feet. A kind of caoutchouc can be obtained from this tree. A still more gigantic fig tree of Queensland is *F. colossea* (F. v. M.), but it may not be equally hardy, not advancing naturally to extratropic latitudes. This reminds of the great council-tree, *F. altissima*.

Ficus elastica, Roxburgh.*

Upper India. A large tree yielding its milk-sap copiously for caoutchouc. Already Roxburgh ascertained 60 years ago, that Indiarubber could be dissolved in Cajaput oil (so similar to our Eucalyptus oil), and that the sap yielded about one-third of its weight caoutchouc. This tree is not of quick growth in the changeable and often dry clime of Melbourne, but there is every prospect that it would advance rather rapidly in any of our extensively unutilized forest gullies, and that copious plantations of it there would call forth a new local industry. Mr. S. Kurz states that also *F. laccifera* (Roxb.), from Silhet, is a Caoutchouc fig tree, and that both this and *F. elastica* yield most in a ferrugineous clay soil on a rocky substratum ; further, that both can bear dryness, but like shade in youth. Several other species of tropical figs, as well American as Asiatic, are known to produce good caoutchouc, but it is questionable whether any of them would prosper in our southern latitudes; nevertheless for the conservatories of botanic gardens, all such plants should be secured, with a view of promoting public instruction.

Ficus rubiginosa, Desfontaines.

New South Wales. One of the most hardy of all fig trees, and very eligible among evergreen shade trees. It is estimated that the genus *Ficus* comprises about 600 species, many occurring in cool mountain regions of tropical countries. The number of those, which would endure our clime, is probably not small.

Flindersia Oxleyana, F. von Mueller.

The yellow wood of New South Wales and Queensland. Other species occur there, among which *F. Bennettiana* is the best for avenue purposes.

Fitzroya Patagonica, J. Hooker.*

Chili, as far south as Chiloe. The Alerce of the Chilians. Grows on swampy moory places. The diameter of the stem reaches sometimes the extraordinary extent of 15 feet. The wood is almost always red, easily split, light, does not warp, stands exposure to the air for half a century, and in Valdivia and Chiloe almost all buildings are roofed with shingles of this tree (Dr. Philippi). Like *Libocedrus tetragona* this tree should be extensively planted in our unutilized swampy moors.

Flacourtia Ramontchi, l'Heritier. (*F. sapida*, Roxburgh.)

India up to Beloochistan. This and *F. cataphracta* (Roxb.) form thorny trees with somewhat plumlike fruits. With other species they can be adopted for hedge copses.

Flueggea Japonica, C. Richard.
China and Japan. The mucilaginous tubers can be used for food, a remark which applies to many other as yet disregarded liliaceous plants.

Fraxinus Oregana, Nuttall.
California and Oregon. Delights on river banks. Wood durable and elastic (Bolander). Well available for planting along our numerous forest brooks.

Garuleum bipinnatum, Lessing.
South Africa. A perennial herb of medicinal properties, and like numerous other plants there and elsewhere, praised as an alexipharmic, but all requiring close reinvestigation in this respect.

Gelsemium nitidum, Michaux.
Southern States of North America and Mexico. A twining shrubby plant of medicinal value, long since introduced into Australia by the writer, like numerous other plants of industrial or therapeutical importance. Active principle Gelseminin. The scent of the flowers has also come into use as a cosmetic.

Gonioma Kamassi, E. Meyer.
South Africa. This small tree furnishes the yellow Kamassi wood, much sought for carpenter's tools, planes and other select articles of wood-work; also for wood engraving, according to Dr. Pappe. Flowers deliciously fragrant.

Grumilea cymosa, E. Meyer.
South Africa. Dr. Pappe describes the wood of this tree as beautifully citron-yellow.

Guevina Avellana, Molina.
Extends from Middle Chili to the Chonos Archipelago. Briefly alluded to already in the list of trees desirable for Victorian forest culture. One of the most beautiful trees in existence. The snowy white flower-spikes produced simultaneously with the ripening of the coral-red fruit. In the cooler southern regions the tree attains considerable dimensions. The wood tough and elastic, used for boat building. (Dr. Philippi). The fruit of the allied *Brabejum stellatifolium* can only be utilized with caution in a roasted state as an article of diet, because it is noxious or even absolutely poisonous in a raw state.

Guilandina Bonduc, Linné.
Widely dispersed through the intertropical regions of both hemispheres with *G. Bonducella L.* Both would be well adapted for hedges in the warmer parts of our colony.

Gunnera Chilensis, Lamarck.
From Caracas to Patagonia, chiefly on cliffs. A most impressive plant for scenic groups in gardens. Darwin measured leaves 8 feet broad and 24 feet in circumference. The acidulous leaf stalks serve as a vegetable; the thick roots are used for tanning and dyeing. *G. macrophylla* (Blume) is a native of Java and Sumatra, where it occurs on mountains, up to 6,000 feet.

Harpullia Hillii, F. v. Mueller.
The tulip-wood of Queensland. One of the most valuable of the numerous kinds of trees indigenous there for select cabinet work.

Heleocharis tuberosa, Roemer and Schultes.
China, where it is called *Matai* or *Petsi*. This rush can be subjected to regular cultivation in ponds for the sake of its edible wholesome tubers. *H. plantaginea* and *H. fistulosa* of India and our own native *H. sphacelata* are allied plants.

Helichrysum lucidum, Henckel. (*H. bracteatum*, Willdenow).
Throughout the greater part of Australia. The regular cultivation of this perennial herb would be remunerative to supply its everlasting flowers for wreaths, just like those of *H. orientale* (Tournefort), from Candia, are largely grown and sold in South Europe to provide grave-wreaths. Furthermore, the lovely *Helipterum Manglesii* (F. v. M.), from West Australia, could for like purposes be profitably reared on a large scale with several other Australian everlastings. Some South African species of *Helichrysum* and *Helipterum* are also highly eligible for these purposes of decoration.

Hibiscus Ludwigii, Ecklon and Zeyher.
South Africa. A tall shrubby and highly ornamental species, desirable also as yielding a fibre of great strength and toughness.

Hierochloe redolens, R. Brown.
Alps of Australia, Tasmania, New Zealand, Fuegia. Like other species of this genus, a valuable fodder-grass of powerful and agreeable scent. It is one of the largest kinds.

Holcus mollis, Linné.*
Of nearly the same geographic range and utility as the preceding species.

Holcus lanatus, Linné.*
Europe, North Africa, Middle Asia. A well-known and easily disseminated perennial pasture grass, of considerable fattening property.

Holoptelea integrifolia, Planchon. (*Ulmus integrifolia*, Roxburgh).

The Elm of India, extending from the lowlands to subalpine regions. A large tree, with timber of good quality. Foliage deciduous.

Hydnum imbricatum, Linné.

In pine forests of Europe. A wholesome mushroom of delicious taste, which we should endeavour to naturalize in our pine plantations. Other recommendable European species are:— *H. erinaceum* (Pers.), *H. coralloides* (Scop.), *H. album* (Pers.), *H. diversidens* (Fries), *H. auriscalpium* (Linné), *H. subsquamosum* (Batsch), *H. lævigatum* (Sw.), *H. violascens* (Alb.), *H. infundibulum* (Sw.), *H. fuligineo-album* (Schm.), *H. graveolens* (Brot.), *H. Caput Medusæ* (Nees), *H. Hystrix* (Fries). These and other edible fungi are given on the authority of Rosenthal's valuable work.

Hymenæa Courbaril, Linné.

Tropical and southern subtropical America. A tree of colossal size and remarkable longevity. Timber hard, extremely ponderous, close grained, used for select wheel work, tree-nails, beams and planks in various machinery. A fragrant amber-like resin, known as West India Copal, exudes from the stem. The beans of the pod are lodged in a mealy pulp of honey-like taste, which can be used for food. The possibility of the adaptability of this remarkable tree to the warmer parts of Victoria needs to be ascertained.

Ilex Cassine, Linné.

Southern States of North America. A tea-bush, to which also remarkable medicinal properties are ascribed.

Ipomæa Batatilla, G. Don.

Cooler regions of Venezuela. The tubers serve as sweet potatoes. Similarly useful *I. platanifolia* (Roem. et Schult), from Central America, and *I. mammosa* (Choisy), from Amboina.

Juglans cordiformis, Maximowicz.

Japan. This species approaches in many respects *J. Sieboldiana*.

Juglans Mandschurica, Maximowicz.

Corea and Mandschuria. This walnut is allied to *J. cinerea* of North America.

Juglans Sieboldiana, Maximowicz.

Throughout Japan, where it forms a large tree.

Juglans stenocarpa, Maximowicz.
From the Amoor territory. Allied to *J. Mandschurica.*

Kœleria cristata, Persoon.
Widely dispersed over the globe. A perennial grass of fair nutritive quality, sustaining itself on dry soil. The closely allied *K. glauca* can be sown with advantage on coast sand.

Lactuca sativa, Linné.
South Asia. The ordinary annual lettuce, in use since remote antiquity. It is not without value, especially as a sedative for medicinal purposes.

Lapageria rosea, Ruiz and Pavon.
Chili. A half-woody climber with large showy flowers. The berries, which are of the size of a hen's egg, are sweet and edible.

Lardizabala biternata, Ruiz and Pavon.
Peru and Chili, south to 37th degree. A woody climber. The berries, two to three inches long and about one inch broad, possess a pleasant sweet pulp. Two other similarly useful plants exist there.

Laserpitium aquilegium, Murray.
Middle and South Europe. The stems of this perennial herb are edible. The fruits serve as a condiment.

Lathyrus sativus, Linné.
Can only be used with great caution, as its frequent or continuous use induces, like *L. Cicera*, paralysis, not only to man, but also to horses, cattle, and birds.

Laurelia aromatica, Poiret.
Southern Chili. A colossal tree, in Valdivia the principal one used for flooring. Wood never bored by insects, and well apt to stand exposure to the open air, far superior to that of *L. serrata*, the *Vauvan* or *Huahuoa*, which tree predominates over *L. aromatica* in the far south of Chili (Dr. Philippi).

Laurus nobilis, Linné.*
Asia Minor. The Warrior's Laurel of the ancients. The leaves are in much request for various condiments, and the peculiar aroma of these bay-leaves cannot be replaced by any others, unless those of *Lindera Benzoin*.

Leyssera gnaphalioides, Linné.
South Africa. A perennial herb of aromatic scent and taste. Much used there as a medicinal tea.

Lespedeza striata, Hooker and Arnott.*
China and Japan. An annual herb, which in North America
has proved of great use. Mr. Meehan states it to be identical
with the Hoop Koop plant, and that it has taken possession of
much waste land in the southern states. It grows there wonderfully on the hot dry soil, and the cattle like it amazingly.

Levisia rediviva, Pursh.
North-West America. The root of this herb is large and starchy, formerly extensively used by the native inhabitants. The plant deserves trial-culture.

Liatris odoratissima, Willdenow.
Southern States of North America. A perennial herb occurring on swampy places.

Libocedrus tetragona, Endlicher.*
Chili as far south as Magelhaen's Straits, especially in moist moory localities. The wood, though soft and light, is resinous and will resist underground decay for a century and more, like that of *Fitzroya Patagonica*; for railway sleepers this timber is locally preferred to any other (Dr. Philippi).

Lindera Benzoin, Blume.
From Canada to the Gulf of Mexico, there called the spice laurel. An aromatic bush, one of the hardiest of the order. The aroma of the foliage much like that of the bay leaves.

Liquidambar orientalis, Miller.* (*L. imberbe,* Aiton.)
Asia Minor. Also this tree yields liquid Storax, which is vanilla scented, containing much *Cumarin,* and thus used for imparting scent to some sorts of tobacco and cigars, also for keeping moths from woollen clothing. Its use in medicine is more limited than in perfumery.

Lotus corniculatus, Linné.* Birdsfoot-trefoil.
Europe, North Africa, North and Middle Asia, extratropical Australia. A deep-rooting perennial herb, readily growing on pasture land, sandy links and heathy places. This plant is well deserving cultivation on light inferior soil, on which it will yield a greater bulk of herbage than any of the other cultivated clovers; it is highly nutritious, and eaten with avidity by cattle. From the great depth to which its roots penetrate, it is not liable to be injured by drought. The nearly allied *L. major* yields a still greater amount of herbage, it is particularly suited for bushy and moist localities, and it attains its greatest luxuriance

on soils which have some peat in their composition (Lawson).
Here in Australia this *Lotus* shows a decided predilection for wet
meadows.

Lotus Tetragonolobus, Linné.
Countries on the Mediterranean Sea. Though annual, this herb
is highly valued for sheep pastures. The allied *L. siliquosus*
(Linné) is perennial, and occurs in a succulent form on sea
coasts.

Lycium Afrum, Linné.
Africa and South-west Asia. Can with many other species be
utilized as a hedge bush.

Lycopodium dendroideum, Michaux.
North America. This, with *L. lucidulum* (Michaux), has become
there a great article of trade, being in request for bouquets and
wreaths, and both plants, after having been dyed of various
colours, are used as ornaments in vases, etc. (Meehan). These
clubmosses are mentioned here to draw attention to similar
plants indigenous in this colony, viz. *L. varium, L. clavatum,
L. densum, L. laterale* and *Selaginellauliginosa.*

Lygeum Spartum, Linné.
Regions at the Mediterranean Sea. This perennial grass serves
much like the ordinary Esparto grass.

Lyperia crocea, Ecklon.
South Africa. The flowers of this shrub produce a fine orange
dye, and are also in use for medicinal purposes.

Maba geminata, R. Brown.
One of the Ebony trees of Queensland. Wood, according to Mr.
O'Shanesy, black towards the centre, bright red towards the bark,
closegrained, hard, heavy, elastic, and tough. It takes a high
polish, and is recommended for veneers. *Maba fasciculosa*
(F. v. M.) has the outer wood white and pink. Several other
species exist in Queensland, which may likely give good substitutes for Ebony wood.

Marlea Vitiensis, Bentham.
New South Wales and Queensland. A middle sized tree,
generally with a gouty trunk; wood bright yellow with fine
undulating rings, black towards the centre. Fruit edible
(P. O'Shanesy).

Marliera glomerata, Bentham. (*Rubachia glomerata*, Berg).
The *Cambuca* of subtropical Brazil. The fruits attain the size of
apricots, and are much used for food (Dr. Rosenthal).

Marliera tomentosa, Cambessedes.
> Extratropical Brazil. The *Guaparanga.* The sweet berries of this tall shrub are of the size of cherries.

Matricaria glabrata, Candolle.
> The South African Chamomile. This annual herb is there in renown as an excellent substitute for the European Chamomile (Dr. Pappe).

Maytenus Boaria, Molina. (*Boaria Molinæ,* Candolle ; *Maytenus Chilensis,* Candolle).
> Chili. An evergreen tree, assuming in the southern provinces considerable dimensions. Wood extremely hard. Cattle and sheep browse with predilection on the foliage; hence the trees are cut down when in protracted snowfalls or in times of drought forage becomes scarce (Dr. Philippi).

Medicago arborea, Linné.
> South Europe, particularly Greece. This shrubby yellow lucerne is of value for dairy farmers, as it much promotes the secretion of milk. This genus includes several other species of pastoral value.

Melia Azedarach, Linné.
> South Asia, North and also East Australia, and there to far extratropical latitudes. As an avenue tree not without importance, because it will successfully cope with dryness of clime and sterility of soil. It recommends itself also for retaining the foliage till very late in the season, and for producing abundance of fragrant flowers. A black fruited similar *Melia* seems as yet little known. The wood is considered of value for some kinds of musical instruments.

Melianthus major, Linné.
> South Africa. The leaves of this stately plant are very efficacious as antiseptics, also in cases of scald head, ringworm and various other cutaneous diseases (Dr. Pappe). Its effect of promoting granulation is very remarkable (Dr. A. Brown).

Melica nutans, Linné.
> The Pearl grass. Europe and North and Middle Asia, enduring an alpine clime, and living also in the shade of forests. It produces suckers, and affords good herbage in woody regions, so also *M. uniflora.* Several other species are on record from various parts of the globe, among which *M. mutica,* of North America, seems to deserve special attention.

Melica ciliata, Linné.

Europe and Middle Asia. A perennial fodder grass, particularly desirable for sheep.

Melicocca bijuga, Linné.

Central America, on mountains. So many sapindaceous trees of the *cupania* series have been shown by my own experiments to be hardy here, that now also this important member of the series could be admitted into this list. The pulp of the fruit is of grape taste; the seeds can be used like sweet chesnuts.

Meriandra Abyssinica, F. v. M. *M. Benghalensis*, Benth.

Abyssinia, on high mountains. A shrub of penetrating odour, utilized much like sage.

Mesembryanthemum acinaciforme, Linné.

The Hottentot fig of South Africa. Under the same vernacular name is also comprised the distinct *M. edule (L.)* Both together with our own *M. æquilaterale* (Haworth), which extends also widely along the American west coast, should be transferred into any of the most inhospitable desert regions, as they afford in the inner part of their fruit a really palatable and copious food.

Milium effusum, Linné.

English Millet grass. Europe, North and Middle Asia, North America. Perennial, suited for damp forest land particularly, the pastoral capabilities of which it enhances. On river banks it attains a height of six feet. It is relished by cattle. The seeds can be used like millet, the stems for the manufacture of superior straw hats.

Mimosa rubicaulis, Lamarck.

India. A hedge-bush, almost inapproachable. It has proved hardy at the Botanic Garden of Melbourne.

Monarda didyma, Linné.

North America. A perennial odorous herb, producing the medicinal Osnego or Beebalm Tea. *M. punctata (L.)* is also of very strong scent, and so *M. fistulosa (L.)* with several others.

Monetia barlerioides, L'Heritier.

South Africa. A hedge shrub.

Moringa pterygosperma, Gaertner.

The horse radish tree of India, abundant into the middle regions of the mountains. The long pods are edible; the seeds are somewhat almond-like and rich in oil. *M. aptera* (Gaertner) occurs from Abyssinia and Egypt to Arabia and Syria.

Morchella esculenta, Persoon. (*M. conica,* Persoon).
Europe, Asia, North and Central America. With *M. semilibera* this Morel has been found in Victoria and New South Wales; its spread should be encouraged by artificial means, as it is a wholsome esculent. European superior species, probably admitting of introduction, are:—*M. Gigas* (Pers.), *M. deliciosa* (Fries), which extends to Java, *M. patula* (Pers.), the Bell-Morel; and several others occur there or in other parts of the globe. Though these fungi show a predilection for pine forests, they are not dependent on them; thus the writer found *M. esculenta* in our Eucalyptus forests, and this late in the autumn. They can all be dried and preserved for culinary purposes.

Morus celtidifolia, Humboldt.
From Peru to Mexico, ascending to 7,000 feet. The fruit also of this Mulberry tree is edible. *M. insignis* (Planchon), from New Granada, is a similar species.

Myoporum lætum, Forster.
New Zealand, where it is called *Ngaio* by the aborigines. As a shelter tree it is equal to our *M. insulare* for the most exposed parts of the coast. It is excellent for shade, and its wood takes a fine polish. It can be raised on the beach from cuttings. Uprooted it will produce new roots if covered in near the sea. Sheep and horses browse on the foliage.

Myrica cerifera, Linné. The wax Myrtle.
Sandy sea-coast of North America. This shrub helps to bind the rolling sand; it has fragrant leaves; the fruits are boiled, and the floating wax, which can be converted into candles, is skimmed off.

Myrica cordifolia, Linné.
South Africa. This bushy plant arrests the influx of sea sand; it also yields remuneratively wax from its fruits.

Myrica quercifolia, Linné.
South Africa. This and *M. cordifolia* and the following are the principal wax bushes there. Many other species from different parts of the globe are available for trial culture, but none has as yet been discovered in Australia.

Myrica serrata, Lamarck.
South Africa. Shrub only about three feet high. The *Myrica* wax is heavier, harder, and more brittle than beeswax, but melts easier. It is obtained from the fruits throughout the cool season. The sowing of seeds is done after the first rain of the cool

months has steadied the sand. The plant can also be multiplied from cuttings. The subterraneous trunk is creeping, and in age of considerable length. (Dr. Pappe.)

Myrrhis odorata, Scopoli. The Sweet Chervil or Cicely.
Mountains of Middle and South Europe and Asia Minor, particularly in forests. A perennial aromatic herb, used for salad and culinary condiments. It could here be naturalized in the forests, and would endure the climate of our highest alps; a second species, *M. occidentalis* (Benth.), occurs in Oregon.

Myrtus communis, Linné.
The Bridal Myrtle. This bush of ancient renown should not be passed, it is industrially in requisition for myrtle wreaths.

Myrtus edulis, Bentham. *(Myrcianthes edulis, Berg.)*
Uruguay. A tree attaining a height of about 25 feet. Berries of 1½ inch diameter, of pleasant taste.

Myrtus Luma, Molina.
South Chili. A tree fully 100 feet high in the virgin forests. Wood very hard and heavy, much sought for press screws, wheel spokes and select implements (Dr. Philippi.)

Myrtus Meli, Philippi.
South Chili. Of the same use as the foregoing species, and in this manner most favourably contrasting with the numerous other myrtaceous trees of Chili.

Myrtus nummularia, Poiret.
The Cranberry-Myrtle. From Chili to Fuegia, also in the Falkland Islands. This trailing little plant might be transferred to the turfy moors of our alpine mountains. Dr. Hooker describes the berries as fleshy, sweet and of agreeable flavour. Allied species occur in the cold zone of the Peruvian Andes.

Myrtus tomentosa, Aiton.*
India and China. This showy shrub ascends to 8,000 feet high. The berries are dark purple, of cherry size, pulpy, and of aromatic sweetness. Various other Myrtles with edible berries are known from different warm countries.

Nageia (Podocarpus) elongata, L'Heritier.
South Africa. With *N. Thunbergi* and with *Ergthrina Caffra* and *Oreodaphne bullata*, this is the tallest tree of Capeland and Caffraria, although it does not advance beyond 70 feet. The yellowish wood is highly valuable, deal like, not resinous. The stems can be used for top-masts and yards of ships.

Nageia (Podocarpus) andina, Poeppig. (*Prumnopithys elegans*, Philippi.)

The *Lleuque* of Chili. A stately tree with clusters of edible cherry-like fruits. The wood is yellowish and fine grained, and is chosen for elegant furniture work.

Nageia (Podocarpus) Chilina, Richard.

The *Manniu* and *Lahual* of the Chilians. Height to 100 feet, with corresponding thickness of stem. Wood white, of excellent quality.

Nageia (Podocarpus) elata, R. Brown.

East Australia. A fine timber tree of great height.

Nageia (Podocarpus) nubigena, Lindley.

Southern Chili, generally a companion of *N. Chilina*, with which it agrees in its dimensions and in the utility of its timber.

Nephelium lappaceum, Linné.

India. This tree furnishes the Rambutan or Rampostan fruit, similar to the Litchi and Logan fruit. As one species of *Nephelium* is indigenous as far south as Gipps Land, and as all the species seem to require rather a moist mild forest clime than great atmospheric heat, we may hope to bring also this tree here in favourable spots to perfect bearing.

Nageia (Podocarpus) Thunbergi, Hooker.

South Africa. Superior in the quality of its wood to *N. pruinosa* (E. Meyer) and even *N. elongata;* it is bright yellow, fine grained and very handsome when polished (Dr. Pappe).

Nyssa multiflora, Wangenheim.

Eastern States of North America, where it is called the Forest Tupelo or Black Gum tree. Wood tough, firm, fine grained, but very unwedgeable (Dr. Asa Gray). It is used for turners' work. Leaves of deep crimson hue in autumn. The acidulous fruits are edible.

Nyssa uniflora, Walter.

Eastern States of North America. The Swamp Tupelo. Wood soft, that of the roots very light and spongy, thus used for corks (Dr. Asa Gray). Attains a height of 80 feet. The mucilaginous fruits are edible.

Opuntia Dillenii, Candolle.

Central America. A Tuna-like Cactus, serving for uninflammable hedges, and perhaps also for the rearing of the *Coccus Cacti*. It is particularly eligible for barren land.

Opuntia Missouriensis, Candolle.
From Nebraska to New Mexico. Mr. Meehan found this *Cactus* covered with the Cochineal Coccus and points to the fact that this insect will live through the intense cold, which characterises the rocky mountains of the Colorado regions.

Opuntia Rafinesquii, Engelmann.
North America. The most northern of all species, extending to lake Michigan.

Osmitopsis asteriscoides, Cassini.
South Africa. A camphor-scented shrub, much in use there for medicinal purposes (Dr. Pappe).

Oxalis esculenta, Otto and Dietrich.
Mexico, there with *O. tetraphylla* (Cavanilles), *O. Deppei* (Loddiges), *O. violacea* (Linné) and several others producing tuberous starchy wholesome roots; the first mentioned gives the largest yield. As similarly useful may be mentioned among many others—*O. crenata* (Jacquin), from Chili, and *O. enneaphylla* (Cavanilles), from the Falkland Islands and Magelhaen's Straits.

Pachyma Hoelen, Fries.
China. This large truffle occurs particularly in the province of Souchong. Flavour most agreeable.

Panax papyrifer, F. v. Mueller. (*Aralia papyrifer*, Hooker, *Fatsia papyrifera*, Bentham, *Tetrapanax papyrifer*, C. Koch).
Island of Formosa. The Rice paper plant, hardy in the lowlands of Victoria, and of scenic effect in garden plantations; the pith furnishes the material for the so-called rice-paper.

Pappea Capensis, Ecklon and Zeyher.
South Africa. The fruit of this tree is of the size of a cherry, savoury and edible.

Pandanus furcatus, Roxburgh.
This screw pine occurs in India up to heights of 4,000 feet, according to Mr. S. Kurz; hence it will likely bear our clime, and give us a stately plant for scenic group-planting. *P. pedunculatus* (R. Brown) occurs in East Australia as far south as 32nd degree, and the same or an allied tall species luxuriates in Howe's Island.

Pelargonium odoratissimum, Aiton.
South Asia. A perennial trailing herb, from the leaves of which a fragrant oil can be distilled. The same remark applies to the shrubby *P. Radula* and *P. capitatum* (Dr. Rosenthal).

Periandra dulcis, Martius.
Subtropical Brazil. The sweet root yields liquorice.

Persea Teneriffæ, Poiret (*sub Lauro*). (*P. Indica*, Sprengel).
Madeira, Azores and Canary Islands. This magnificent tree produces a very beautiful hard mahogany-like wood, especially sought for superior furniture and turners' work. One of the most hardy trees of the large order of *Laurinæ*.

Peucedanum Sekakul, Bentham.
Egypt and Syria. Biennial. The root is edible.

Peucedanum cachrydifolium, Ledebour.
Persia. A valuable fodder herb (Dr. Rosenthal).

Peumus Boldus, Molina.
The Boldo of Chili. A small ornamental evergreen tree, with exceedingly hard wood, which is utilized for many kinds of implements. The bark furnishes dye material. The fruits are of aromatic and sweet taste (Dr. Philippi).

Pisonia aculeata, Linné.
Tropical and subtropical countries of both hemispheres, extending as a native plant into New South Wales. This rambling prickly bush can be chosen for hedge copses.

Pithecolobium dulce, Bentham.
Mexico. A valuable hedge plant. The sweet pulp of the pod is wholesome.

Pittosporum tenuifolium, Banks and Solander.
New Zealand. This with *P. eugenioides* has proved exquisite for tall garden hedges, for which these and several other species were first brought into notice by the writer. Our native *P. undulatum* is rather adapted for copses, and deserves cultivation also for the sake of its fragrant flowers, from which an essential oil can be distilled.

Planera aquatica, Gmelin.
North America. An elm-like tree, which can be chosen for plantations in wet localities.

Plectronia ventosa, Linné.
South Africa. A hedge bush like *P. ciliata* (Sonder) and *P. spinosa* (Klotzsch).

Poa Abyssinica, Jacquin.
The Teff of Abyssinia. An annual grass. The grain there extensively drawn into use for bread of an agreable acidulous taste.

Poa Canadensis, Beauvois.
  The Rattlesnake grass of North-East America. A valuable swamp grass.

Polygala crotalaroides, Hamilton.
  Temperate Himalaya. Praised as an *ophidian alexipharmic*. To several other species both of the eastern and western hemispheres similar properties are ascribed, but we are almost entirely without any reliable medical testimony on these and many other vegetable antidotes against snake poison.

Polygaster Sampadarius, Fries.
  South Eastern Asia. One of the most palatable of all truffles.

Polygonum tinctorium, Loureiro.
  Japan and China. An annual herb, deserving attention and local trials here, as yielding a kind of Indigo. Its growth would be vigorous.

Prunus ilicifolia, Nuttall.
  California. In deep rich soil valuable for evergreen hedges of intricate growth.

Prunus Mahaleb, Linné.
  Middle and South Europe. It deserves some attention on account of its scented seeds and also odorous wood, the latter used in turnery for pipes and other articles.

Psidium acidum, Martius.
  Higher regions on the Amazon river. A tree, 30 feet high; its guava fruit pale yellow and of apple size.

Psidium chrysophyllum, F. von Mueller. (*Abbevillea chrysophylla,* Berg.)
  The *Guabiroba do mato* of South Brazil. This tree attains also a height of about 30 feet. The fruit generally not larger than a cherry. Perhaps other species of the section *Abbevillea* would be hardy here and worthy of cultivation.

Psidium lineatifolium, Persoon.
  Mountains of Brazil. Berry about 1 inch diameter.

Psidium malifolium, F. v. Mueller, (*Campomanesia malifolia,* Berg).
  Uruguay. Berry about one inch diameter.

Pterocarpus Indicus, Roxburgh.
  The Lingo of China and India. A tree of considerable dimensions, famed for its flame-red wood. It furnishes also a kind of dragon blood resin.

Pterocarpus Marsupium, Roxburgh.
India, ascending in Ceylon and the Circars to at least 3,000 feet altitude; hence this tree would doubtless grow without protection in those tracts of our colony which are free of frost. It exudes the best medicinal kino, which contains about 75 per cent. of tannic acid. *P. santalinus* (Linné fil.), which provides the Saunders or red sandal wood, is also indigenous to the mountains of India.

Pterocarya fraxinifolia, Kunth.
Central Asiatic Russia. A kind of walnut tree, which with *P. stenoptora* (*Cas. de Cand.*) on Dr. Hance's recommendation, should be adopted as trees for both ornament and timber, and so perhaps also the Japanese species.

Punica Granatum, Linné.
The Pomegranate. North Africa and West Asia. Well-known for its showy habit, rich coloured flowers, peculiar fruit, and medicinal astringency, but much overlooked regarding its value as a hedge plant.

Pyrus Japonica, Thunberg.
Japan. One of the prettiest of small hedge bushes. Under favourable circumstances it will produce its quince-like fruit.

Pyrus nivalis, Jacquin.
The Snow Pear. Middle and South Europe. This would be adapted for orchards in our higher mountain regions. The fruit becomes soft and edible through exposure to snow. *P. amygdaliformis* (Villars) is probably the wild state of this tree.

Pyrus salicifolia Linné.
Greece, Turkey, Persia, South West Russia. Though its fruit, which slowly mollifies, is edible, this tree is mainly utilized as a superior stock for grafting.

Quercus densiflora, Hooker and Arnott.
Californian Chesnut Oak. A large evergreen tree of beautiful outline, dense foliage and compact growth. Bark very valuable for tanning; wood however subject to rapid decay (Prof. Bolander). *Quercus Douglasi* and *Q. lobata* are two other tall oaks of California.

Quercus lobata, Nee.
California. The large acorns can be used for food.

Quercus lyrata, Walter.
The overcup Oak of the south-eastern states of North America, extending from South Illinois to Florida and Louisiana. Lately recommended as one of the most valuable for timber cultivation.

Quercus Phellos, Linné.

The Willow Oak of the Eastern States of North America. The acorns available for food, like those of several other species, for instance, *Q. glabra* (Thumb.), of Japan. The comparative value of the very numerous cis- and trans-atlantic Oak, is but little as yet understood, either for avenue purposes or timber plantations, and should be tested with care in botanic gardens. Even recently oaks have been discovered on the mountains of New Guinea.

Raphanus sativus, Linné.

South Asia, up to 16,000 feet in the Himalayas, eastward to Japan. *R. caudatus* (*L.*), the radish with long edible pods is regarded by Dr. Th. Anderson as a mere variety, and he thinks that all sprung from the ordinary *R. Raphanistrum* (*L.*) of Europe.

Rhamnus Græcus, Reuter.

Greece. From this shrub, and to a less extent from the allied *R. prunifolius* (Sibth.), are the green dye berries collected in Greece, according to Dr. Heldreich. These shrubs grow on stony mountains up to 2,500 feet.

Rhus caustica, Hooker and Arnott.

Chili, where it is called the Litre. A small or middle-sized tree, the very hardwood of which is used for wheel-teeth, axletrees, and select furniture. The plant seems neither caustic nor otherwise poisonous (Dr. Philippi).

Royenia Pseudebenus, E. Meyer.

South Africa. Only a small tree, but its wood jet black, hard and durable, thus in Capeland and Caffraria called ebony. *R. pubescens* (Willd.), according to Dr. Pappe, furnishes there a wood adapted for xylography; this may give a clue to the adaptability of many other kinds of woods in the large order of *Ebenaceæ* as substitutes for the Turkish box-wood.

Ruscus aculeatus, Linné.

Middle and South Europe, North Africa, South-West Asia. This odd plant is the only shrubby species of the genus. It serves for forming garden hedges. The young shoots of this and others are edible.

Rubia peregrina, Linné.

Middle and South Europe, South-West Asia. This perennial species yields also Madder-root. Several other kinds deserve comparative test culture.

Salix Capensis, Thunberg. (*S. Gariepina*, Burchell).

South Africa. This willow might be introduced on account of its resemblance to the ordinary weeping willow. *S. daphnoides* (Vill.) of Europe and Asia, *S. petiolaris* (Smith), *S. cordata* (Muehlenb.), *S. tristis* (Aiton), of North America are among the best for binding sand. *S. longifolia* (Muehlenb.), also North American, is among those which form long flexible withes.

Salix Humboldtiana, Willdenow.

Through a great part of South America. This willow is of pyramidal habit, attains a height of 50 feet and more. The wood is much in use for yokes and other implements. Many kinds of willow can be grown for consolidating shifting sand ridges.

Santalum album, Linné.*

India, ascending to the temperate elevations of Mysore. A small or middle sized tree, famed for its fragrant wood and roots. In the drier and stony parts of ranges the greatest fragrance of the wood is generated. *S. Freycenetianum* (Gaudichaud) produces sandal wood on the mountains of the Sandwich Islands, up to 3,000 feet. Several other species occur in Polynesia. The precious sandal oil is obtained by slow distillation from the heartwood and root, the yield being about 2½ per cent.

Santolina cyparissias, Linné.

Countries at the Mediterranean Sea. A very aromatic and handsome bush, of medicinal value. There are several allied species.

Saxono-Gothæa conspicua, Lindley.

The *Mahin* of Southern Chili. A middle-sized tree, with fine-grained yellowish timber.

Sassafras officinale, Hayne.

From Canada to the Gulf of Mexico and the Missouri States. The greatest height attained by this tree is 50 feet. It furnishes the medicinal Sassafras bark and wood, and from this again an essential oil is attainable. The deciduous and often jagged leaves are remarkable among those of Lauraceæ.

Scandix grandiflora, Linné.

Countries around the Mediterranean Sea. An annual herb, much liked there as a salad for its pleasant aromatic taste.

Scorzonera crocifolia, Sibthorp.

Greece. A perennial herb; the leaves, according to Dr. Heldreich used there for a favourite salad and spinage.

Scutia Indica, Brogniart.
   South Asia. This, on Dr. Cleghorn's recommendation, might be introduced as a thorny hedge shrub.

Selinum Monnieri, Linné.
   From East Asia now extending to South Europe, preferring moist places. An annual herb, praised by the Chinese as valuable for medicinal purposes.

Smilax rotundifolia, Linné.
   Eastern States of North America and Canada. A prickly climber with deciduous foliage. An immense local use is made of the roots for the bowls of tobacco pipes, clay pipes being there almost unknown. It is estimated that nearly three millions of these briar-root pipes are now made a year. The reed portion of these pipes is generally prepared from *Alnus serrulata* (Meehan).

Solanum Fendleri, Asa Gray.
   New Mexico. A new kind of potato, enduring a temperature of zero. Mr. Meehan's endeavours to obtain good sized tubers have as yet not been successful. The following plants are also spoken of by Dr. Rosenthal and others as new kinds of potato, perhaps to be developed through cultivation : *S. demissum* (Lindley), *S. cardiophyllum* (Lindley), *S. utile* (Klotzsch), *S. verrucosum* (Schlechtendal), *S. Bulbocastanum* (Dunal), *S. stoloniferum* (Schlechtendal), all from Mexico, and some from elevations 10,000 feet high ; *S. Maglia* (Molina) from Chili, and *S. immite* (Dunal) from Peru.

Sophora tetraptera, Aiton. *Var. Macnabiana,* Graham.
   The Pelu of Chili and Patagonia. A small tree with exceedingly hard and durable wood, much used for cog-wheels and similar structures. The wood differs much from that of *S. toramiro* of the Easter Island (Dr. Philippi).

Spartina cynosuroides, Willdenow.
   Eastern part of North America. A perennial grass of fresh water swamps, there often called prairie grass ; it can be utilized for fodder, and its value as paper material seems equal to that of *Esparto.*

Spinifex hirsutus, La Billardière.
   On the whole coast of extra-tropical Australia. Highly valuable for binding coast sand with its long creeping roots.

Spinifex longifolius, R. Brown.
   On the tropical and western extra tropical coast of Australia. Available like the former.

Spinifex squarrosus, Linné.
>India. Useful like the two preceding plants. Tennent remarks that the radiating heads become detached when the seed is matured and are carried by the wind along the sand, over the surface of which they are impelled by their elastic spines, dropping their seeds as they roll along. The heads are so buoyant as to float lightly on water, and while the uppermost spiny rays are acting as sails, they are carried across narrow estuaries to continue the process of embanking beyond on any newly formed sandbars.

Spondias dulcis, G. Forster.
>Fiji, Tongan and Society Islands. This noble tree is introduced into this list to indicate, that trials should locally be instituted here as regards the culture of the various good fruit bearing species of this genus, one of which *S. pleiogyna* (F. von Mueller) transgresses in East Australia the tropical circle. The lamented Dr. Seemann saw *S. dulcis* 60 feet high, and describes it as laden with fruit of agreeable apple flavour called Rewa, and attaining over 1lb. weight.

Streblus asper, Loureiro.
>South Asia. This bears a good recommendation for live fences, it being a shrub of remarkable closeness of branches.

Swietenia Mahagoni, Linné.
>The mahogany tree of West India. The degree of endurance of this famous tree is not sufficiently ascertained. In its native mountains it ascends to 3000 feet.

Synoon glandulosum, A. de Jussieu.
>New South Wales and South Queensland. This evergreen tree deserves cultivation in sheltered warm forest valleys of our colony, on account of its rose-scented wood. Some species of *Dyszoylon* of East Australia produce also rosewood.

Tagetes glanduligera, Schranck.
>South America. This vigorous annual plant is said by Dr. Prentice to be *pulicifugous*.

Tamarix articulata, Vahl.
>North and Middle Africa, South Asia. Of similar utility as *T. gallica*. The same or an allied species extends to Japan.

Tamarix Germanica, Linné.
>Europe and West Asia. Likewise available for arresting the ingress of shifting sand, particularly in moist places, also for solidifying precipitous river banks.

Tamarix Gallica, Linné.*
South Europe, North and tropical Africa, South Asia. This shrub adapts itself in the most extraordinary manner to the most different localities. It will grow alike in water and the driest soil, and is one of the most grateful and tractable plants in culture ; it is readily multiplied from cuttings, which strike root as easily as a willow, and push forth stems with unusual vigour. Hence it is one of the most eligible bushes for planting on coast sand to stay its movements, or for lining embankments.

Taraxacum officinale, Weber.
Dispersed over most of the temperate and cold parts of the globe, but apparently not a native of this part of Australia. This well-known plant is mentioned, as it can be brought under regular cultivation to obtain the medicinal extract from its roots. It is also considered wholesome to pasture animals. The young leaves furnish a medicinal salad.

Tarchonanthus camphoratus, Linné.
South Africa. This bush deserves attention, being of medicinal value. As an odorous garden plant it is also very acceptable.

Tectona grandis, Linné fil.
The teak of South Asia. This superb timber tree has its northern limit in Bandalkhand, at elevations of 2000 feet, which circumstance may encourage test-culture here.

Terminalia Catappa, Linné.
India, ascending mountain regions. Few trees, as stated by Roxburgh, surpass this in elegance and beauty. We have yet to learn whether it can be naturalized here, which it especially deserves for its nuts. Several species extend in East Australia to subtropical latitudes. The seeds are almond-like, of filbert taste and wholesome. The astringent fruits of several other species form an article of trade, sought for a lasting black dye. *T. parviflora* (Thwaites) forms a large tree in Ceylon, at elevations up to 4000 feet.

Tetranthera Californica, Hooker and Arnott.* (*Oreodaphne Californica,* Nees.)
Oregon and California, where it is called the Mountain Laurel or Bay tree. On the banks of rivers attaining a height of 100 feet, throughout pervaded by a somewhat camphoric odour. Wood hard, close grained, durable, susceptible of a high polish, easily worked. used for superior flooring, turnery and manifold other select work. The tree is easily cultivated, and of comparatively quick growth (Dr. Behr and Dr. Bolander).

Tetranthera calophylla, Miquel. (*Cylicodaphne sebifera*, Blume.)
Mountains of Java and the Neilgherries. From the kernels of
the berries a tallow-like fat is pressed for the manufacture of
candles. The yield is comparatively large. Trial cultures with
this tree might be instituted in our humid forest valleys.
T. laurifolia (Jacq.) of tropical Asia and Australia and *T. japonica*
(Sprengel) are noted as similarly utilitarian.

Thapsia edulis, Bentham. (*Monizia edulis*, Lowe.)
On the island of Deserte grande, near Madeira, where it is called
the Carrot tree. It might be of some use to bring this almost
shrubby umbellate to the cliffs of our shores; though the root is
inferior to a carrot, perhaps cultivation would improve it.

Theligonum cynocrambe, Linné.
Countries around the Mediterranean Sea. An annual spinage
plant of somewhat aperient effect.

Thouarea sarmentosa, Persoon.
Tropical shores of the eastern hemisphere. This curious and
tender grass might be easily introduced, to help binding the sand
on sea beaches.

Tilia argentea, Desfontaines.*
The silver lime-tree of South-east Europe. The wood is not
attacked by boring insects. The flowers are deliciously
fragrant, and yield on distillation a precious oil.

Tinguarra Sicula, Parlatore.
In the countries at the Mediterranean Sea. The root is edible
and celery-like.

Tristania conferta, R. Brown.
New South Wales and Queensland. A noble shady tree, attaining a height of 150 feet. It is not only eligible as an avenue
tree, but also as producing select, lasting timber; ribs of vessels
from this tree have lasted unimpaired 80 years and more.

Triticum junceum, Linné.
Europe and North Africa. A rigid grass with pungent leaves
and extensively creeping roots, requiring sea sand for its permanent growth. One of the best of grasses to keep rolling sand
ridges together, and particularly eligible where cattle and other
domestic animals cannot readily be prevented from getting access.

Triphasia Aurantiola, Loureiro.
South-east Asia. This shrub is worth cultivation for the
exquisite fragrance of its flowers. The fruits though small are

of pleasant sweetness. The plant may prove also adapted for hedges. *Glycosmis citrifolia* (Lindley), and *Claussena punctata* (Oliver), also both East Asiatic fruit shrubs, may possibly show themselves hardy in our sheltered forest regions.

Tropæolum tuberosum, Ruiz and Pavon.
Peru. The tuberous root serves as an esculent.

Tuber albidum, Fries.
Occurs with *T. æstivum*, but is smaller and less agreeable in taste. The means for transferring truffles and any other edible fungi from one country to another, require yet to be further studied and finally devised, but they appear quite feasible.

Tuber magnatum, Pico.
Grey Truffle. South Europe. One of the most esteemed truffles, with some garlic flavour.

Tuber rufum, Pico.
Red Truffle, especially in vineyards. Much used for food, but smaller than the *Terfezia* truffles.

Ulmus crassifolia, Nuttall.
The evergreen Elm of Mexico and Texas.

Ulmus montana, Withering.
The Wych Elm. Europe and extratropical Asia. Attains a height of 120 feet.

Ulmus Mexicana, Planchon.
Cordillieres of North America. This elm attains a height of 60 feet or perhaps more.

Ulmus pedunculata, Fougeraux. (*U. ciliata*, Ehrhart.)
Europe and Asia, through their middle zone. A fine avenue tree.

Ulmus parvifolia, Jacquin
The evergreen elm of China, Japan and Queensland. A similar tree is found in the Himalayan Mountains.

Vigna lanceolata, Bentham.
Tropical and subtropical Australia. Mr. O'Shanesy observes that this twiner produces, along with the ordinary cylindrical pods, others underground from buried flowers, and these somewhat resemble the fruit of Arachis. The plant is available for culinary purposes.

Villebrunia integrifolia, Gaudichaud.

India, ascending the Himalayan mountains to 5,000 feet. A small tree, allied to the Rami plant, *Boehmeria nivea*. Mr. C. B. Clarke regards the fibre as one of the strongest available in India, it being used for bow strings. Other *Villebrunias*, for instance *V. frutescens*, and also some species of *Debregeasia*, particularly *D. velutina*, deserve likewise regular culture, for the sake of their fibre. Moist forest tracts seem particularly adapted for these plants, because *V. integrifolia* grows in Sikkim at an elevation where, according to Dr. G. King, the rainfall ranges from 100 to 200 inches. This fibre is much more easily separable than that of *Maoutia Puya*, according to Dr. King's observations.

Witheringia solanacea, Helrit. South America. This perennial herb needs trial culture, on account of its large edible tubers.

Zelkova crenata, Spach. (*Planera Richardi*, Michaux).

South West Asia, ascending to 5,000 feet. In favourable localities a good sized tree, with qualities resembling those of the Elms. The allied *Z. cretica* (Spach) is restricted to South Europe.

Zizyphus Lotus, Lamarck.

Countries around the Mediterranean Sea. The fruits are small and less sweet than those of *Z. vulgaris*; nevertheless they are largely used for food in the native country of this bush.

Zizyphus Sinensis, Lamarck.

China and Japan. Similar in use to the last.

Zizyphus Spina Christi, Willdenow.

Middle and North Africa, South West Asia. Rather a hedge plant than a fruit bush.

Zizyphus Joazeiro, Martius.

Brazil. Recommended as yielding fruit in arid regions.

OSTRICH FARMING.

The following interesting letter and enclosed report on the subject of Ostrich Farming was received some time ago by Dr. Thomas Black from Sir Henry Barkly. It was accidently omitted in Mr. Samuel Wilson's paper on the Ostrich in last year's proceedings. As Dr. Atherstone's report may prove of interest to many, it is now published.

"Government House, Cape Town,
June 11, 1872.

"My dear Sir,—When I wrote to you by H.M. ship Dido, on the 14th ult., with reference especially to the desire of the Acclimatisation Society of Victoria to procure information as to the proper management of domesticated ostriches, I mentioned that I had asked the aid of Dr. W. G. Atherstone, the well-known naturalist of Graham's Town, but had not yet received his notes on the subject. These notes reached me a few days since, and I have now the pleasure of transmitting them for the use of the Society.

"I think they will prove very useful, as Dr. Atherstone has taken an opportunity of talking the matter over with Mr. Dunn, formerly of the Victorian Geological Society, and has made suggestions based on what he has been told of the soil and climate of your colony.

"The enclosed advertisement will show you where the artificial hatching machines alluded to are to be procured, and I will only repeat that I shall be happy to assist the Society, if necessary, in importing one.

"Believe me, in great haste,
"Yours very truly,
"Dr. Thomas Black."   "HENRY BARKLY.

The advertisement enclosed is one by Mr. A. Douglas, of Bilton, near Graham's Town, offering artificial hatching machines for sale. The following is Dr. Atherstone's report:—

"This new and important branch of industry is beginning to attract considerable attention here, and deserves the serious consideration of all interested in the welfare of the colony. The export of feathers is rapidly increasing every year in quantity and value, not so much, I believe, from wild feathers, indicative of the progressive destruction of the ostrich, as from the increase of the domesticated birds and their more successful management, by which the feathers at one time considered vastly inferior to those of the bird in its wild state, are now proved by market value to be equal if not superior in quality. I have, myself, seen, during the last 18 months, upwards of 500 domesticated ostriches in different districts of the colony in the Eastern and Western Provinces, under varying conditions as to soil, climate, and management, some in enclosures, some herded in large flocks like sheep, without enclosure or shelter of any kind; and, from my own observations and the inquiries I have made, I am of opinion that the success of ostrich farming, like that of sheep farming, depends more upon the character of the veldt (or soil and grazing ground) and diet than upon climatic conditions. Exposure to wet and cold does not appear to be injurious to birds in full health and vigour, but it kills them if weak or out of condition. It is advisable, however, to protect them by shelter of some kind from the cold rains of winter in the domesticated state. The natural home of the ostrich and antelope is found in the Karroo plains and sweet grass flats of the interior, and although, like the springbok, the ostrich occasionally resorts to the long sour grass of the coast lands, where, perhaps, the lime and salt replace alkalies of the 'sweet grass' and Karroo, neither will thrive for any length of time on the 'strand veldt' or the 'sour grass' of the sandstone ranges, deficient in alkalies. Alkalies in some form or other seem to be necessary to the very existence of sheep, bucks, and ostriches, and where these do not exist on the soils or plants, they must be supplied artificially to ensure the healthy condition of the animal, and the proper growth of the wool, hair, and feathers. It is for this reason that salt, so necessary for all domesticated animals, is in some parts of the Brazils said to be worth its weight in gold. I have heard of a house, the walls of which (made of brack ground) were nearly licked through by a span of tuurveldt oxen let loose on the reef. The attraction of the salt licks or pans in the interior for game and stock is well known. This natural want may often be recognised at a glance on the surface of a farm. No bones are seen lying about on a tuurveldt farm, all being greedily devoured by the stock; cattle and sheep crush them up, and ostriches swallow them whole, whereas on a sweetveldt farm, whose soil and shrubs are rich in alkalies, the bones are untouched. Nothing requires them. There are three farms adjoining each other within a dozen miles of Graham's Town, on which upwards of 150 ostriches are kept, which strikingly exemplify this fact, and this comparative adaptability of different soils and pasture for sheep, Angoras, and ostriches. Kruisfontein, on the south, belonging to my brother, John Atherstone, is an unmitigated tuurveldt farm situated on the sandstone range called the Tuurberg, which skirts Graham's Town on the south. There is no limestone on the farm. He has been at considerable expense in sheds, enclosures, and artificial feeding, and though successful at last, it has been only attained by dear-bought experience; Angoras do not succeed, and, as a rule, wethers only thrive well, lambs are reared with difficulty, and ostriches require a large amount of artificial food, mealies and green crops, and require crushed bones, which they devour greedily. Until this plan was adopted, the birds were in low condition, unhealthy, and the feathers inferior and interrupted in their growth.

"Since the supply of bonedust (he gives ¼lb. sulphur to two buckets of crushed bones with salt) the improvement in the quality and value has been very marked, and the condition of the birds greatly improved. The yield and quality of the feathers appear to be directly proportionate to the health and vigour of the bird. Limestone, from the coastland, was tried at first, as the birds would not lay; it was broken up and scattered about, but the birds would not touch it, the phosphate of lime of the bones was the thing wanted, and they rushed at the bones with avidity, and immediately began to improve in health and to lay. Still, although he has had ostriches for nearly three years, and began with many full-grown birds, the attempts at incubation have been abortive from various causes, and he has had no increase. Of 85 birds originally placed on the farm in a 400-acre enclosure, he has lost 27—13 by cold and wet, three by diphtheria, six killed by natives, three by fighting, and two by falling into holes; he has five more males than females. Of 60 eggs, 19 were destroyed by black crows, which were seen from the house to hover over the nest and let stones fall on the eggs (on running up on one occasion to the nest, about 600 yards off, he found three stones in the nest, the eggs cracked, and the yolk strewed about); 41 were sent to the adjoining farm, Hilton, to be artificially incubated, but these failed, probably from having been shaken, although they were carried in baskets on the heads of native women. He has received £1,450 for his feathers, plucking them every eight months, selecting the ripe feathers only, and plucking about sixty at a time. He finds it injures the bird and produces irritation fever to pluck too many at once. His experience leads him to the opinion that the ostrich cannot stand exposure to wet or cold. This farm is rather higher (about 200 ft. or 300 ft.) than the other two, and therefore, perhaps, colder. The next farm, Hilton, is like the table farm adjoining it, on the junction between the sandstones of the Lunberg and the schists and trap conglomerate formation, mixed veldt, partly sour and partly sweet grass—the soil rich in alkalies, which often effervesce on the surface, in the hollows. On Hilton, Mr. Arthur Hughes has now 71 birds, kept in an inclosure of 300 acres, in good condition and requiring very little artificial food. They lay well, and do not appear to suffer from exposure to wet or cold, although they have no shelter. He commenced about three years ago with eleven birds; he has now 71; he has successfully hatched 70—40 artificially in the incubator. They have paired and hatched their young in the natural state, which has enabled him to watch them, and he has thus acquired much valuable informa-

OSTRICH FARMING.   101

tion regarding their habits and the natural mode of incubation. The male birds are very ferocious during the breeding season, and it is dangerous to approach them. Mr. Douglas has had several very narrow escapes. They sit alternately, the male at night grazing and guarding the female. During the daytime, the time of the male bird going on the nest varies during the period of incubation, as also does the time between the female leaving the nest and the male taking her place, the exposure and cooling being probably regulated by the temperature of the incubation fever at different stages. All these apparently trivial minutiæ are yet matters of considerable importance in artificial incubation, and only to be acquired by patient watching and judicious application of the principles involved in machine-hatching. " Black Kloof," which adjoins Hilton on the N.E., is on the trap conglomerate—a purely sweetveldt farm—with many of the bitter and aromatic shrubs of the Karroo. Here Mr. George White, my brother-in-law, has 23 young ostriches in an enclosure of 500 acres, thriving well, in good condition, and yielding feathers of excellent quality. As a rule he gives no artificial food; they thrive and fatten on the scanty scrub and sweet grass in the enclosure only. Last year, when he put several hundred sheep and goats into the same enclosure, the birds were nearly starved, but they regained their condition as soon as the sheep were removed. They have no shelter of any kind, and have not suffered at all from rain or cold. He began with seven—four males, and three females, all chicks, their sex undistinguishable from the plumage. He has had them 16 months, and has not lost one. He plucks them twice a year. In rainy weather they do not even seek the slight shelter of the walls, but group themselves in the open ground, not appearing to care for cold or wet. The rocks, soil, and herbage contain alkalies in abunance, and the water is brackish, as the name of the farm implies. Sheep and Angoras and cattle thrive well, and no bones are eaten by the stock ; they lie scattered about everywhere. The contrast between the farms is very marked, and their comparative fitness for ostrich farming. Ostriches require, as a rule, I think, 'sweetveldt' variety of food, and a large extent of grazing ground to roam over, to keep them in health and vigour."

"The Wimmera district, as I am informed by Mr. E. J. Dunn, geologist, who is intimately acquainted with the district, is ill adapted to the successful rearing of ostriches, although when reared they may thrive very well with artificial food. Mr. Dunn, who has lately travelled a good deal in our colony, and knows the peculiarity of our sweet and sour veldts, recommends the banks of the Loddon, near Baringhup, as better adapted for experimental ostrich-farming ; it is, he says, sweetveldt, and the high banks and the rich flats along the river, and the high banks and stony ground above it, are more likely to suit the birds ; the lucerne also growing luxuriantly there, which is one of the best green crops for ostriches. My brother gives 200 lb. to 300 lb. lucerne daily to his birds, besides mealies, or Indian corn (1 lb. to each bird). With regard to plucking the feathers, which unfortunately are in prime condition at the period of incubation, when the plucking of them would interfere sadly with the birds, different opinions are entertained some pluck, some cut off the feathers close to their insertion, some separate some of the males from the females about the time of incubation, and then pluck them. My own opinion is that the best plan is that adopted by a farmer in the Western District, who had 70 or 80 ostriches, and found the plan the best and most convenient. To show me the process, he had the whole flock driven in, and we then insinuated ourselves by wriggling amongst the densely packed birds. He had previously shown me what to do in case of any bird proving vicious—they are perfectly in your power if you seize them by the neck, you may then choke them as far as you please until you find them powerless, and you can then run away. Having got with my friend into the middle of the crowd, so packed that they were unable to move, he quietly selected two or three of the best feathers, and with a curved sharp knife in his right hand, the blade protected by lying flat against his finger, he pressed it down as near the root as he could, and cut it off obliquely upwards. The bird was quite unconscious of the operation, standing perfectly still as he handed several to me; he then picked out a blood feather, very beautiful, which on being cut, bled a little, but the sharp knife separated it without it being felt. In a month or six weeks he took out all the stumps, if they had not already fallen out. By this means the health of the bird is not impaired, no irritation fever is produced, as in the case of my brother's birds, and you can select the feathers that are in prime condition, leaving the others to ripen in due course. Still the process of incubation injures a great many valuable feathers, and it appears, therefore, clear to me that some mode of artificial incubation must be attempted to derive all the advantages possible from this new branch of industry. I therefore wrote to my son in London, about three years ago—early in 1869, I think—requesting him to hunt up some maker of incubators for hens' eggs, hoping, by giving him the size of the egg, habits of ostrich, &c., to be enabled to get a machine adopted for hatching ostriches. He sent me a letter in reply, and prospectus from Mr. W. H. Thick, 188 Weddington-road, Kentish Town, London, W.C., offering to construct one if I sent him all particulars. I had great difficulty in inducing anyone to enter on the risk. My brother declined, preferring to wait till he saw if his birds would not breed in their natural state, and hatch their young. Not being a farmer myself, although perceiving at once the immense value of such an important aid to this second diamond discovery or rather gold discovery to the colony (for feathers were realising their weight in gold—£45 per lb., and single feathers, 15s. to £1 each, or about £60). I could not myself carry out the idea. At last I persuaded Mr. Arthur Douglas, of Hilton, to send home an order for one of Mr. Thick's machines, which, on the road from Port Elizabeth, was unfortunately broken to pieces. However, by constructing another on the same principle, which was afterwards varied to suit the new phenomena that presented themselves during the experimental incubation, and taking advantage of the practical lessons of the birds actually on the nest, testing their temperature, &c., Mr. Douglas has succeeded in making a machine which has proved very efficient, though in many respects differing from the one originally imported. Several ostrich farmers have had his improved incubator, and have been perfectly satisfied with their success. It is astonishing what slight causes will cause the failure of eggs; a thunderstorm has been known to destroy them; even the rough opening of the drawer containing the eggs will shake and injure them, and too great or too little heat proves fatal to the chicks. By this plan, one male to three females is sufficient; in a natural state of course there must be an equal number, as both sit alternately. I saw large herds of ostriches near Colesberg, 150 in a flock at least, herded by only two men on horseback with long whips on open flats. I presume mealies tempted them to the homestead in the evening, where they remained on the 'reef' until the next morning. I enclose a *Farm* of Nov. 10, 1870, with Thick's letter.

" W. G. ATHERSTONE."

www.ingramcontent.com/pod-product-compliance
Lightning Source LLC
Chambersburg PA
CBHW031408160426
43196CB00007B/949